SUE ORTON

Gathering Threads a memoir

Copyright © Sue Orton 2023
Published in 2023 by Sue Orton
The right of Sue Orton to be identified as the author of this work has been asserted by her in accordance with the Copyright, Designs and Patents Act 1988.

All rights reserved.
No part of this publication may be reproduced or transmitted in any form or by any means, electronic or mechanical, including photocopy, recording or any information storage and retrieval system, without permission in writing from the publisher.

British Library Cataloguing in Publication Data
A catalogue record for this book is available from the British Library

ISBN: 978-1-80352-786-4
Design and Print Management by Pete Goddard
www.goddard.graphics

Printed by
Newman Thomson Ltd

With love and thanks to Sarah Quantrill

To all my birth family
my mum, my dad and my sister Jane.

Thanks as well
To Catherine Dudley, a warm hand on my back.
To Neill Thew, who loved me before I did.
To Noelle Branagan, a wonderful friend.
To my insightful niece Sarah Nute.
To Anna Barrick, my treasured craniosacral therapist.

To Lulah Ellender, writing mentor.
To tutors and colleagues on Creative Writing Programme:
Creative Non-Fiction 2020-22.

For Hélène Clay
writer, poet & musician
a brilliant encourager, critic and ally
1969 - 2023

2022

Prolific is anchored off the south coast of the Isle of Wight. Where Sarah, my long love, grew up. A special place for her. It's calm, sunset, a beautiful evening. Restful after a challenging 24 hours. I am on board an Ocean Youth Trust boat on a trial cruise to see if I might be recommended as sea staff. This year I feel so alive. Happy. Joyful. Full of energy. I'm in my late 60's with a new hip and hearing aids. Could I cut it? We had been at sea for a few days. I was in the deck house with the skipper and mate. Both women. Sharing stories.

"Do you think I could ever work as sea staff with OYT?"

"Of course you could ... "

"Not could, but you should? Absolutely! You are an inspirational woman."

"I am?"

1999

I was scared of fireworks, Bonfire-nights, until the millennium. Fingers in my ears.

"I'll be in the car until it's over."

Then in 1999 something changed.

"Southsea Castle should be a good place to see the Millennium fireworks all round the bay. Are you coming?"

"Yes ... yes I'll come."

I had just agreed to go to possibly the loudest, longest firework display ever seen or heard. Could I cope?

To my astonishment at midnight as the cacophony began, I stood there. Holding hands with Sarah, my new girlfriend. No fear, no panic. I loved it. I turned to her, she knew my apprehension, I shouted:

"It's amazing, I'm NOT scared. I love it. I bloody love these fireworks!"

PROLOGUE

I was born in Radcliffe, Lancashire, a loved wanted child. Second sibling, four years waiting. A sunny disposition. Inquisitive, intelligent, intuitive. But something wasn't right. I felt I was born in the wrong place. The North. My mum was always correcting my speech.

"Butter has a t Susy! Not bu'ur. Speak properly!"

"We'll have to send you to boarding school to get rid of that accent.

"Lancashire accents are working class and we don't want people thinking you are that."

"You will go after Jane. It will be four years after."

"Oh."

My parents and sister moved to Bury, Lancashire from idyllic Chichester before I was born. I felt their loss and sadness. No sailing, just boring golf clubs and Bridge. No sea. My parents. A love match in wartime. Dad of Indian Empire sensibilities, 'home' to boarding school at eight, charming, certain and arrogant. An architect trained each side of a north Atlantic convoy in WW2. Met my mum aged nineteen in Yeovilton, third daughter of a teaching family. She was intelligent, book loving, with a practical love and talent for painting, sculpture and mischief. Kind and gentle. After the war they chose to settle in Chichester, West Sussex. Coast, sea, friends, sailing, home. They loved it. Their first child Jane was born into a mum painted Mickey Mouse nursery. It was a happy friendly, time and place. They all thrived.

Then loss of work, drove them reluctantly north to a family paper mill in need. Elton Paper Mill. Duty. Loss. Stepping away from a creative, colourful, playful life. To the North. A paper mill by the polluted stinking Irwell River. Working class grime. Dad put his drawing board in his cramped sweaty office and never used it again. My mum followed him and had an allowance. I think she was very lonely.

Our big house was isolated down a two mile lane with cobbles, only a farm nearby. Later I would walk this lane to school with my grey hat hidden in my satchel. Silently deeply, I swallowed a belief that duty trumps creativity. Heavy and depressing duty sat solidly on inspiration. Two creative people putting down their joy for duty. The north. The mill. The wrong place. My home. I swallowed duty, the silent loss and tried to stay sunny. A tomboy certainly. Creative yes that too, but how difficult is it to sense the early days of our instincts?

I remember Garsdale fondly, home, with my bike, my dungarees, my sister, walking dog Tarka to the mill ruins with her then later alone, jumping from block to block along the stinking Irwell River heady with Rosebay Willow Herb. Alive, adventurous, inquisitive, until first my sister, then I was sent away to boarding school at eleven.

I think it was well intentioned, probably to get rid of that accent and stop me being northern and to make sure I became a proper girl. A potential wife, what else was there? A servant of the men of the empire. Friendly, confident, capable. Serving. Unaware of the hidden agenda then, I looked forward to going. I tried. But it wasn't me.

I was to discover slowly, silently, painfully that I was different. So, imperceptibly, with deadly stealth, I denied myself and was lost, until I didn't know who I was. I think I tried hard to be the daughter they wanted but in the process I gave myself away. I became tangled. I split myself in two. Wandered. Conformed. Struggled. Worked. Then the slow long road out.

Now in my late 60's I am untangled, whole. Safe. At last. Here in my studio at my desk, coffee in hand, I am attempting to unpack, unravel and make sense of my journey to this all embracing soul-deep happiness. To map my untangling.

I am following the threads that caused a difficult, powerful life changing event to happen to my body over 18 months from March 2019 - July 2020; I shed a skin. I'm looking into my life trying to understand where the trauma, the rash, the debilitating thick yellow hard dry cracking, bleeding layers on my hands and feet, the stickiness of my legs and arms, sleepless nights, the red patches on body, face and neck, was started, was seated, was hiding. Where the threads of confidence and courage lay which held and healed me. It seems very likely to me now that my body, the cells in my body, had silently trapped and moulded my closet experiences into hidden bodily trauma. Shedding through the skin is a process known by therapists to be a helpful way for long buried trauma to rise and be released. So, perhaps what happened to me was a very natural unnatural process.

Threads feel long and thin like mycelium. Some trying to hide, like I was, and others more visible. Strong, creative, professional. Post shedding, I feel at last, as if the whole of me is in the world. So I am tracking back, to the source, to the moments, to the tears and into the joy. Now a proud, happy, partnered, creative lesbian. It's been a long road. Untangling and gathering my threads. Confronting a difficult past. Let's see what I find.

EARLY DAYS

Cattle grid. Cobbles. Setts in Lancashire. Bigger than my shoes.

"I'm off with Tarka down to the ruins, mum."

My early childhood exploring derelict mills and rivers with a black Labrador. Mud and cows delighted me. Dungarees and wellies. Running and hiding. Playful. Out of the garden gate over the old bent cattlegrid.

"Don't stand on the cracks or the bears will get you."

Turn right down the cobbled road to the old derelict village. Calrows. A row of two up two downs and a shop. I could only just look over the counter.

"Ey up, what can I get ya?

"Can I have one liquorice lace, please?"

"That'll be a penny, duck."

"Thanks."

"Ta rah."

"Ta rah."

Down the road to bends in the river. Looming to our right an old mill, four storeys. Dark empty holes for windows. Built of blackened stones as big as me. Spooky. Could I hear the clackety clack of mill looms? A little hop and skip, shiver, look around and dash down the canal path before they caught me! Heart racing we reached a derelict bridge. A challenge.

"Hey Tarka, which planks shall we go over the canal today?"

The wooden beam, slippery; the wood and metal girder, easy; or the metal girder, narrow scary. Usually I chose the metal girder. I liked a physical challenge.

Before boarding school I only remember living at Garsdale, Calrows, Bury, Lancashire. No post code. I moved there when I was two. I was a small person, balanced on my feet, secure running. I was born loved and wanted, my mum told me. My bedroom was cosy and warm, the opposite end of the house to my sister. When my father moved his mistress and her daughter into Garsdale after my mum was thrown out, he gave my room away. I never really forgave him for that. I didn't say anything because I loved my dad.

Garsdale was isolated down a lane with cobbles. It had fields all round it with cows. I liked cows. They would push their large black noses through the hedge and I would touch them with my small hands. Noses bigger than my hands, damp soft with a little pattern all over them, wet, warm, inquisitive. A cattle grid, bent poles from many cars, guarded our drive. I never saw a cow trying to get over it. I would tiptoe round the edge holding onto a wooden fence and bushes. There was a laburnum tree which had dangly yellow flowers in the spring. I collected the flowers to decorate my bike, pushing the stems into the soft handle-bar ends. I knew nothing of their poison.

No-one lived near us except the Entwhistles who owned the farm and the cows. The farm was over the road from Garsdale at the junction between cobbles and tarmac. I would go to the farm with Jane to get eggs and milk. All the hens were in big cages and the smell made me hold my nose.

There was a little landing space outside my bedroom door overlooking the stairs, just by my mum and dad's room, they had two beds. My father had a high chest of drawers behind the door with a bowl on the top for the loose change he kept in his trouser pocket. He also had a crumpled bit of paper with my writing on it:

"I, Susy Orton, will never, ever, ever, wear make-up or paint my nails," signed Susy aged 7.

Garsdale was a large house. It had a hall with wooden floors and rugs with patterns on them from India. It had a big staircase with a massive window of small panes looking out onto the drive. It had scary bits. There were gremlins. Especially in the upstairs lavatory. In the water box high on the wall behind the pan. There was a chain to pull. I ran downstairs before it finished and caught me. I had a strategy.

Door, open for escape. Wee. Pull up my pants. Ready ... Crouch down, knees flexed. Poised. Climb on the pan lid. Reach up on tiptoe to the chain. PULL. Jump down. Run. Down corridor to top of stairs. Sharp right turn. Slide. Wooden stairs. Slippery. Leap stairs two to three at a time to mid landing, 180 turn and slide ... and jump ... slide landing on the hall rugs ... sliding to a halt in the sitting room. All before the flush finished. Safe.

One day, my dad stuck a mirror about the size of my open hand in the downstairs cloakroom. He put it at my height, small, so I could see myself. There was a mirror at adult height above it, but he knew I couldn't see into it. I was a bit of a tomboy. I didn't want to be a boy, although maybe my father wished I was. He probably missed his brother Bill, who was shot down while a passenger in an aeroplane in the 1940's. He never talked about him. He also had a sister, Ciss. I found all their names in the Aldeburgh Sailing Club year book for 1938-9. Sailing was his passion.

I wanted clothes I could run in and be with the cows. Dungarees or chunky trousers. Difficult to find for girls. My mother helped me search. Jane recently found a photograph and sent it. She has written in small, perfect 9 year old white chalk script.

"Mum and Sue taken by me 'Garsdale' Feb 1958."

I was five. Mum is leaning on a familiar wooden small garden gate. 'Lean-on-easy and gaze out' sort of size for an adult. Behind her, a familiar remembered paved yard. Washing on the line and the top of a pear tree that I remember her planting. I am in front of the gate, looking down. My arm on the gate top and left leg raised slightly on the low bar. Casual. I had on my perfect outfit. Long sleeved knitted jumper round neck with a collar peeking out of the neck. Trousers. Soft cotton woven stripes, not bold, with a square pocket. Comfortable. Easy going. I have a music festival pair in my wardrobe now!

Mum would take me to Bury market. I loved the bustle and busy-ness of the market. I loved cooked beetroot and fish. Still do.

"... 'addock, Cod, 'ake, fresh fish straight from the trawlers in 'ull."

"... come on ... four for sixpence, any fruit you want!"

I had a fabulous suit of plastic grey armour, helmet, breastplate, shield and a sword. My helmet had a visor, my breastplate a buckle round the back and I could hold my sword with my shield and run. I loved to run. Sometimes my visor came down while I was running across the fields. One day friends with an Irish wolfhound were visiting. He was in the field too.

"Do you think Susy has seen Laird running towards her?"

"Probably not as her visor is down."

"Oh ... I think they may collide ..."

I loved that suit. Another photograph from my sister. Me sitting on a pony, in my armour, at my Uncle Phil's house. Posh. Horses. Green baize door to the kitchen. Jane has written on the back:

"This is probably the first picture of Susy fighting the good fight."

When I was five I went to school for the first time. Beechfield School. Miss Lee was my first class teacher. Beechfield was behind Gigg Lane, the football ground for Bury football club. I would spend much time watching football there later in my life but today I was more concerned about Miss Lee.

She was tall and stooped in the loft room, our classroom. We had small battered desks with inkwells and no ink. I was sad, a silent, quivering, not very sure, not looking up, sort of sad. Lost, nervous, small, alone. Small behind a small well scratched wooden desk, each with its years of small grubby insecurities and spelling tests scratched on the lid.

"Susan Orton, what are you crying for?"
"I want my sister ... "
"Don't be silly, she is in her own classroom, get on with your work."
" ... I want my sister ... "
... eventually Miss Lee relented and took me into my sister's classroom. I stood at the front, snivelling.

My sister's bedroom was at the other end of the house from mine. Her bed was tucked under a sloping roof with a window that looked out onto the drive. There was a plant that grew up into the roof so big it was in the roof space white and ghostly. The octopus. She often had her head in a book and I was always running about. When she came home from boarding school, I couldn't wait to go and see her. I remember standing just outside her door, slightly trepidatious, wondering, hoping, liking just being here, near her, not sure why, that deep love forged thread. Garsdale doors were black thick wooden doors with curly latches that were too big for my hands. A curved tongue shaped latch at the top, it was hard to grasp, I had to go on tip-toe to reach and then curl both hands round the handle and swing to press the tongue down to lift the latch to get them open. I used to make her midnight feasts of sandwiches and take them to her room. I spent my pocket money and bought a full life size set of pictures of The Beatles for her birthday. I wonder where they are now.

Jane was always there ahead. Four years ahead. Until she disappeared one day to go to boarding school. Walks down to the ruins, up to the waterfall. I wonder now how it was for her, how we were? She played chopsticks on the piano with dad, I tried. I asked Jane recently for her memories of Garsdale when we were children. We made plaster cast models in cups, I remember being careful pouring in the white liquid plaster into the legs, heads and arms, upside down in a cup, then carefully unpeeling. Jane was there ahead. An unconscious constant. An ally. Older than me, taller than me, with pig-tails. She was ferocious. Tearing Pamela Wrigglesworth's dress in my defence.

"My sister is NOT a cry baby, she's only just started school."

"Leave her alone!"

Over the cattle grid onto the cobbles, climb the gate into the field, running together down to the river. Into the ruins, big stepping stones of the derelict factory, jumping gaps, daring gaps, slippery gaps, laughing. She is my only sister and I love her. We did fight though too.

"I want ... "

"No, that's mine ... "

"No it's not, I took it first ... "

"You didn't ... I did ... ! I did, I did!!"

"No you didn't ... just give it to me."

"Ahhh ... please!!!

"No!!"

"Mum! ... Janes took my ... Susy just hit me!"

After Beechfield I went to Bury Grammar School, the junior bit. Grey uniform. Felt grey hats. A mile walk down the lane, down the dip to the main road. A tuppenny bus ride. Hopscotch on the playground. Little bottles of milk at break.

"We will be having a spelling test every Friday, the *Friday Test*."

"Yes Miss Hamilton." we chorused.

I dreaded Thursday evenings.

"Susy, have you learnt your spellings for your Friday spelling test?"

"Mmm not sure ... Can I play outside?"

"Yes when you've learnt them ... "

"Must I?"

"Yes, you will never pass your common entrance without spellings."

Vehicle: verkicle? no Susy there's no r or k, there's a silent h. Ve... hic...le. I still remember it like that.

Most days I would get the bus and then walk the lane home from school. I had a trick to save tuppence on the bus

"On you get now, upstairs you youngsters."

I noticed the bus conductor took tickets from downstairs first ... I waited until he was on his way upstairs. Busy, preoccupied. Squeezing past him ...

"I need to get off here ... please."

"Yes!"

I was a physical child. I learnt to swim in Bury Municipal Pool. Slippery floors and wet changing rooms. Chlorine. Big curving stone steps into the pool.

"Susy just stay on the top step where you can stand. I know you are safe as you can float and swim a few strokes. I won't be long."

I liked to explore ... I would float at the top and then hold my breath and swim underwater down to the bottom and come back up. Pulling myself up each step until I bobbed to the surface and I could stand on the top step. Time and again.

"Look mum, I can swim! If I hold my breath I can swim to the bottom and back up!"

"What are you doing? You have to learn to swim on the top of the water first!"

Later, we had school swimming races with a starting gun. I didn't like bangs. Balloons. Fireworks or guns. I had my fingers in my ears. The gun went, I took them out of my ears, dived in late and won the race.

SCULPTURE

One day my mum told me to meet her after school at Bury Art College.

"Where is it mum?"

"It's next to the library and museum. Where you borrow the Narnia books you like and next to the museum with the model boats."

"I know. Where will I find you?"

"I'll be in the studio with Miss Childs doing sculpture."

Four o'clock the next day.

"My mum's in a studio doing sculpture, where do I go please?"

"Along the hall and down the stairs. The double doors on the left. Be careful as you go in because it's a bit messy in there. All the clay and stuff."

I couldn't see my mum at first. Then I heard her laughter.

"This is such fun, it's so messy."

"Try and get clay-slip into all the cracks of the sculpture ... you'll need three layers."

"Oh Susy, put your satchel over there by the door and you can come and watch."

"What are you doing ... is that plaster like we used in the rubber mould figures at home?"

"Yes it is but different. I'm making a mould around the clay head I have been working on, and this is Miss Childs who's my tutor."

I watched, fascinated. My mum, laughing, smiling, messy ... making a sculpture.

"What happens when you have covered both sides?"

"We leave it to dry and next week I take both sides of the plaster off the head, very carefully ... then take out the clay head, wash it lots of times until it's ready to be a mould for casting."

"But won't you loose the head if you take the clay out?"

"No ... the mold becomes a negative of the head so I can pour new plaster into the hole and make a sculpture."

"Gosh, that's clever. Like the rubber moulds we've used?"

"Well yes, Susy, but your mother has created a beautiful original work in clay and now she will be able to make a model of it in plaster that will last."

"Oh that's brilliant."

This was to prove a pivotal memory in my own creative development. I still have that sculpture in my garden.

WEAVING

In 2016 I completed a Weaving Diploma and designed a South Downs Tweed. One piece had found its way to be seen by a poet and writer who I didn't know. In 2017 she saw it and wrote to me. Much later I sensed this might be a thread of internal confidence building within me. It was a year before any signs of my rash, but internal rumblings perhaps.

"I just wanted to say how utterly beautiful I found your weaving. I sat and looked and looked at it - it compels attention and time in the same way as the landscapes that inspired it. I kept seeing colours floating beneath which changed the colours on top, wanting to see where the threads came from, holding for a moment all the colours together in my mind's eye, then losing them into their separateness. What an encounter. It made me want to write a poem in response, an evocation that I also get from landscape and some paintings. I've never experienced that with cloth before, so thank you. What you do in your weaving is really quite special."

A weaving commission from her partner for a Christmas present soon followed.

It's difficult to isolate the threads of my creative longings and desires. My memory of seeing mum in sculpture class after school laughing? It had always seemed impossible to follow these small isolated yearnings ... but eventually I did. Most of my life slimy skinned, not used to swallowing praise, I was used to slipping away from the positive.

That 2017 Christmas I breathed it in. Swallowed my worth, felt my heart swell with pride and smiled a lot. My shell shivered.

SOUTH

My family often headed south for summer holidays. The pull was strong. Sea. Coast. Sailing. Chichester and my mum's family. We stayed with Gran and Grandpa on Hayling Island and visited Chichester, our real 'home' often. The beach was a bike ride away down Staunton Avenue. The journey. Eight hours in the car, leaving after my dad finished work. Down the middle of England. Old roads. Jane told me stories because it was a long way.

"Are we there yet? "

"No Susy, we are still in Lancashire."

"Shall I tell you how dog roses get their name?"

I loved listening, but usually fell asleep before we left Lancashire.

"Wake up girls, you can see the lights of Portsmouth Harbour. We are nearly there."

It was the middle of the night. Gran's house was called West Gate. They had a lawn, a swinging seat with a fringe, a guinea pig with wiggly orange fur, an asparagus bed, a kitchen smelling of apple pie and a front room they never used. I slept in a room near my Gran and Grandpa's room. At night sometimes I woke up to shouting …

"It's all right Eric you don't have to go over the top, you are having a bad dream."

The First World War had left its mark. My dad felt it too.

"It's because of my father's experience on The Western Front with his Indian Regiment that I swore never to join the army. When the war came again I joined the Navy instead."

Cheney's grocery shop was next door. It had a high counter and shelves. The man there had a long pole with a grabber on the end.

"Gran do we need any cornflakes at Cheney's?"

"No dear I don't think so ... why do you want to go there?"

"I like it when he reaches for the cornflake box with the pole, grabs them and catches them as they fall."

"Why don't you get a box of cupcakes?"

"Orange and lemon ones or chocolate."

"Get chocolate dear, Grandpa likes them."

"Oh but they are more difficult."

"More difficult?"

"Chocolate ones are too gooey, it's much harder getting the paper off without breaking the zig-zag edge."

We had bikes at Gran's house. Dad organised bike rides with cousins on the beach at low tide. Flat, long, sand, perfect for formation riding. He pretended he was directing aeroplanes like when he was in the Navy. Before I could ride on my own I sat on the very small metal seat behind him, with my arms around his waist helping with directions.

"All bicycles line astern!"

I pointed behind ... a wiggly line formed

"Echelon, two rows, right!"

I swayed and pointed my arm firmly to the right causing my dad to wobble and lurch right ...

... two hesitant rows formed

"Arrow formation from me, port and starboard!"

... everyone hung back either side of my Dad to try and work out the instructions ...

"Bicycles, in formation, turn to the right."

... all heading for the sea ...

"Bicycles, in formation, turn to the left."

... the sand dunes.

"All bicycles slow and dismount"

I loved it.

Later I discovered that my mum had ridden a bicycle in formation as a Wren when she met my dad. Her bike had a screen on it so she couldn't see where she was going and trainee fighter direction officers had to shout instructions to her to get to a fixed point, pretending to aim at a submarine. My father was an instructor there. Perhaps they fell in love in formation?

Of course we went to Chichester. Three families. Dear, dear friends. It felt a long way from Hayling Island and a lifetime away from Bury. My home.

'We all lived in flats in the centre of town. In West Pallant. John and Barbara [Towers] were in one flat and we were in another. It was such fun."

The pull and friendships made in Chichester were strong and abiding. I didn't know it then but Catherine Towers was to become a deeply important thread for me. Invisible, strengthening, tangible later.

In September we went back north.

"How long will the journey to Malvern take mum?"

"A few hours I think. It's quite a long way."

There was sadness in her voice. It made me wonder if she was happy about me going. She had argued with my dad for us to go to boarding school. She didn't often stand up to my dad's argument.

"Girls don't need a proper education like boys."

The British Empire didn't rate women.

"They do. If we had boys you would not hesitate to send them to Charterhouse."

"Of course."

"So we will find a good girls' boarding school for the girls."

Malvern Girls' College. One of the best.

"Susy can take the Common Entrance exam in the sitting room at the same time as her 11+ and if she passes she can go."

I'm ten years old in the sitting room in Garsdale. Sitting on a small chair with a folded desk in front of me. Common Entrance and 11+. Dad called it the drawing room sometimes because ... well because my dad called it that.

"Dad, where were you born?"

"India, in a place called Simla. Your grandfather was a Brigadier General in the Indian Army."

"Oh."

"What was it like?"

"I was only there until I was nine, then I was sent home to go to boarding school. My first school was Bowden House School, Seaford, Sussex."

My dad had been sent 'home' alone to a school that was preparing him for ruling the empire. He came 'home' from India with his elder brother and sister. He never went back.

"What do you remember?"

"I had a nanny. I called her my Ayah. She looked after me. One day there was a tarantula on my bed and I asked her to come and get rid of it. She brought a biscuit tin to scoop it up. It had baby spiders in a sack which broke as she scooped and they ran out all over the tin. Then she put the lid on.

"Ahhh... that's scary."

In 1990 after my father's final stroke and before he died. He wanted his Ayah to look after him.

The sitting room was where we had serious family conversations, exams and where we put the Christmas tree. It's where visitors came to sit and have drinks from the cupboard we called the 'rosewood glory'.

"Mum, can I do drinks for Anne and Andrew ... please?"

"I think your daughter is a little too generous with the sherry, Jenny. But I don't mind!"

The sitting room had french windows onto the terrace into the garden. And the lawn.

"Susy your dad is home from the mill."

"Can we go and play catch and save the boundary dad?"

"Yes... give me a minute to get my coat off."

"Have you found the tennis ball?"

"If I stand with my back to the rose bed I will throw it and you can get it before it goes into the hedge... "

"OK, ready ... "

"You are a fast runner... throw it back to me ... accurately now as I can't move much."

"Again... again...

"Supper's ready you two"

I was really accurate as he couldn't move much because of the arthritis in his hips. This would stand me in good stead when I went to boarding school but I didn't know then.

There was an old Indian rug on the floor with animals in lines round the sides. I could slide on it, but I wasn't supposed to. There was a fireplace with a gas fire and white lines between the bricks. I wrote important names on the white lines at different places. Jane, Susy, Tarka, Rocky and Rollo. Tarka was a black labrador and Rocky and Rollo the ginger cats. I took Tarka for walks by myself down the ruins by the river. Once Tarka ran into a stake on the bank by the drive and had to have his chest shaved and stitched up, I think he nearly died. I was very sad.

Waiting to take my common entrance sitting alone at a folded desk in the sitting room. I wonder why it was so important to sever all the links from my home, my life and for me to be taken away to Malvern a long way from Garsdale, where I would learn to be brave and independent. Just like my dad. Jane was there so I wanted to go there too. Common entrance… the exact opposite of common... a lie, a brazen lie, it was not common at all. It was the devil's entrance to a place that would change my life forever. Conform to society. Such manipulation. Such rubbish. So painful.

Jane's godmother said:

"Boys are sent to boarding school so they can go and run the Empire without feeling any emotion."

SAILING: THE FAMILY PASSION

My dad was always talking about sailing.

"Sailing was all we did in the summer holidays before the war."

"Where was that dad?"

"In Aldeburgh in Suffolk. We didn't go home to India. Bill and Ciss were there too."

"Bill and I reduced changing for dinner down to 10 minutes from coming home wet."

I found their names recently in the Aldeburgh Sailing Club year book for 1939. There they were, in the year books, kept in a drawer in a dusty sail loft. Found, treasured and delighted in by an elderly boat builder.

"Your dad was it, sailed here?"

"Yes I think so, before the war. His brother and sister too."

"Well I'll be. Let's have a look then. We might find 'em if we're lucky."

"Ah, here we are. This might be them. I told 'em they were worth keeping. The loft doesn't get much use these days. It's all machines, fibreglass and kevlar. The old skills are leaving us."

"Mind yourself, now, it's dusty up 'ere and I don't want your clothes getting spoiled."

"I've never 'ad a call to look at the old club books before. I knew they were worth keeping. Since the clubhouse fire in the 1970's so much has been lost. It's a good thing I kept 'em."

"Now, when do you think it will be? Here's the 1938 and 1939 books. I think they stopped printing them after that for a while. What were their names again?"

"William Orton, Richard Anthony Orton and Cecily Orton."

"Ah yes, here they are."

Water equalled boats and sailing. My dad told me about his racing. Using terms I didn't yet understand. Tacking and gybing. He always wanted to win and he did, often. I think he was probably quite good, until he had arthritis and couldn't move much. Chichester Harbour and races at Itchenor Sailing Club seemed always to be there. I think he missed the south.

"Once I was sailing in the Firefly National Championships at Itchenor. A week's racing. I only had to win the last race ... It was a stiff breeze. " Wow ... mum were you crewing?"

"No I was pregnant with Jane so Ciss crewed."

"Did you win dad ... ?"

"No ... we were just leading at the weather mark even though we were a lightweight crew. I knew that as we bore away onto the reach we would be away."

"What happened?"

"As we rounded the mark I slid aft to bear away onto the plane and the boat took off. It just flew ... we were in the lead ... then as I went to lean out further I missed the toe strap and fell overboard ... leaving Ciss with an out of control planing Firefly!!"

"Did she recover it?"

"No Ciss capsized ... and the rescue boat team nearly knocked me out with a life buoy. They refused to take me back to the boat so we had to retire."

He built a wooden dinghy for us in Bury. By hand, With plywood. Limping.

Wind off the waterworks. Mud. Competitive sailing. Round and round. He built a wooden boat in the mill workshops. Deep in the factory past steaming sheds and hissing pipes to a warm workshop. A Graduate dinghy. All wood. Planed, cut, stuck, fashioned beautifully. Marine plywood. Endless hours. Days. Shaping, polishing. We took it to Elton. Dropped it off the concrete slip. Went sailing. Getting in and out of a boat. In my blood early.

"Step carefully into the centre of the boat as if there are eggshells."

"Feet apart and flexed knees."

"Sit in the middle, lightly."

"Always, one hand for you and one for the boat"

This early introduction set me up to sail with my cousin on holiday at Mengham Rythe Sailing Club in Oops, a Heron dinghy. Chris was two years older than me.

My dad tried hard to replace the joy of the open water of Chichester harbour sailing. Elton Reservoir sufficed. Small brown concrete edges. Cows in the fields. Wind off the waterworks. Mud. But very competitive sailing. Round and round. His arthritis, already painful. The loss of his mobility in sight. Unspoken anger. Days. Shaping, polishing. He called her Faun for his little dears. She had a sheltered life. Dropped into the water off a rough hard slip. Sailing round and round. No freedom. No sea. Grey skies. Faun. I was seven. I learnt the basics of sailing there. I remember. Tacking and gybing. Keeping your head down from the boom. Jumping out near the shore with the painter. Holding the boat head to wind to get sails up and down.

On a recent sailing holiday as we sailed two Lasers in the soft Mediterranean breeze. Sarah asked

"When did you learn to sail?"

"When I was seven."

Which method did you use for tacking?"

"My dad's"

I needed a trunk. Mine was blue with wooden bars around it and a flap up lock. Jane had a green trunk. It was big. I could lie down in it, like a coffin. And there was the list. Four pages, small typed, expensive, exclusive, exact list. Recommended outfitters for uniform. Skirts x 2 ...

"Skirts!"

"Do I have to have everything on the list?"

"Yes, everything."

"Are those labels for me?

"Yes"

"Why does it say Susan Orton MMO11?"

"That's a code for your house. The Mount. You will live there when you first go."

"Will I know anyone?"

"Not at first. But Jane has been there for four years. She will be the head girl when you arrive."

"Will I be able to see her?"

"I'm not sure, I hope so, you will have to wait and see."

"Can I take Dindy?"

"No dear. You have to leave Dindy behind."

Dindy was my soft, precious constant rag doll, who I used to leave in the raspberry patch and cry for at bedtime. We slept together rubbing cheeks. She couldn't come to MGC. She was not on the list. No line for: one small cuddly inanimate creature who you love, to comfort you. So I left her in Garsdale. I don't have her any more. I lost her when my parents split up in the 1970's.

That first journey, even that first time, I remember very little. Over the cattle grid, cobbles and tarmac. Manchester onto the M6. Through Birmingham. No M5 then, so junctions and roundabouts; junctions and roundabouts. Jane was with me. My mum was there too. Always my dad driving in his pointed pale blue Rover 2000. Fast.

"Are we nearly there?"

A familiar question from the back of the car. We made many long journeys. Every summer, I go to my Gran and Grandpas house in Hayling Island for the holidays.

"The first thing you will see is the line of hills in the distance. The Malvern Hills."

"You will be walking on those every Sunday after church, Susy."

"Will you come with me?"

"I might, but more likely with other senior girls in our house."

"I'm Head Girl now."

The Mount was in Albert Road South, Great Malvern. MMO11. I had labels sewn onto every item in my trunk.

"We are nearly there, Susy."

"Which house is it?"

"The big white one there up the drive."

"You walk down to the Main Building from here every day."

Parking up the drive, we all stepped out. Silent. Big doors, big steps. I was still a very small person following my sister. Tiles on the hall, those small triangles of brown, cream, green or blue, perfect for sliding. Forbidden. Stepping in, walking in. Nervous. The hall was big. The House Mistress. Tall, big skirt, buttoned up blouse and cardigan, glasses with a string

"Ah Mr and Mrs Orton, Jane, welcome back. Head Girl this year."

"And this must be Susan. Welcome to The Mount Susan. I'm sure you'll be very happy here."

"Your trunk will be taken to your dormitory."

"Here is your dormitory leader. Run along now."

Walked away. I looked at my mum, hesitating ...

"Off you go Susan, your parents have a long journey and you will see them again at exeat in six weeks."

"Will she be alright Dick?"

"Yes of course. She'll be fine. I was fine when I was sent home from India to Prep school and I was only nine."

My dormitory was at the top of the back stairs on the right. Eight beds. Cream, metal hoops with wire frames and mattress. I had the one by the wash-hand basin.

"What do I do now?"

"I'll show you where all your clothes and things go so you can unpack your trunk."

No Dindy.

Later. Much later after a silent meal and unpacking. Games boots, hockey and lacrosse stick in the cloakroom. Wash things in a rack by my bed next to the wash-hand basin. All my clothes, somewhere. I had black canvas boots with studs on them for winter games. I was the only one who cleaned them. After brushing off the dry mud, cloth in hand I would put thick black cream on them. They looked smart. I think my hands held my silence then. They held my experiences close. I am only now realising just how much they held me. We couldn't hold hands then so they led a solitary life in my pockets and gloves. There was not much craft then I can remember, learning was all with our heads.

Holding my lacrosse stick, left hand at the bottom of the stick at waist height, holding tight for twisting and right hand at chin height guiding. I loved it.

Would I remember where everything was?

I lay in my bed, the post with a curtain round the basin was by my left ear. Close. Packed in tight. Silent after lights out.

"What are you crying for?"

"I want my sister ..."

"Don't be silly, your sister is the Head Girl, she hasn't time for a snivelling sister."

She came to see me. I know she tried to comfort me but I expect I was snivelling and an inconvenience for her. She had probably toughened her heart, surviving alone in that place.

Four years apart is too long for sibling closeness. Jane my 'dearest elder sister.' Much later Jane began to sign 'des' on her birthday cards to me. Three letters. Yes! I would reply with 'dys'.

SOUTH DOWNS WALK

On this day I walked on the South Down with Jane. Four years older. A big gap. I think she felt it. I felt it. Different lives. We had rarely walked alone together since our childhood. My walk with her in May 2017 triggered my reflection. I realised that since childhood I had never truly seen or felt Jane's care.

"Four years is too far apart Susy. I told my children if they wanted a family not to leave four years between them, it's too much."

For most of my adult life I have found Jane a bit remote and distant. I have struggled to get close to her. I feel it within myself, in my body somewhere, it's not a conscious thing but an ache. We are very different I tell myself, it is because we have had different lives, I'm a lesbian and she is straight, she has children and I don't. I have blamed her, I have thought it was something I did, I thought she was frightened of my sexuality. We argued over mum and blamed each other, sharp barbed.

"Who's having mum for Christmas? It's always me!" "I've had mum on my doorstep since the day I was married, you haven't"

Since she left to go to boarding school, when I was seven, I have never been really, really sure of Jane's love. Demonstrably sure. Hugging sure. Yet that day in 2017 I felt it. Right there. I was ready to feel it too, perhaps. We were trudging the hill together, muddy, slipping, sometimes silent but together. After our South Down walk we had lunch in a low ceilinged, wooden floored, dog friendly pub. Close. Warm. Sisters together. A cord spliced. Fine thread. Important.

MORE SCHOOL

"When the bell goes in the morning you have ten minutes to get up, wash and dress."

"Go to the top of the back stairs and join the queue to go down to breakfast."

MM011 was to be my home for six years. Twelve weeks there. Home. Dindy. Pack trunk. Leave Dindy. Two or three weeks at home. Pack Trunk. Leave Dindy. Drive to Hayling Island for the summer. Home. Drive. New dormitory. Twelve weeks. Pack trunk. Forget Dindy. So I did. No Tarka. No cows. No mum or dad. No cattle grid or cobbles. After that first year, no sister. She moved on to Oxford to take her A levels. I was alone.

I saw signs of my mum at mealtimes. Item 46 on the trunk list was: Napkins x 4. Labelled Susan Orton MMO11. We used them every meal. A basket on the sideboard in the dining room contained them. They were all white linen, except mine. I might have been embarrassed ...

"Your napkins look different. We've all been given proper white linen ones."

"I like mine ... cos they're different and I can find them easily."

Mine were yellow and green striped. My mum chose them. They were beautiful, colourful, individual. I loved them and I loved my mum for her choice. I wonder now if in her loss and sadness she sensed my creative soul and gave me a lifeline of colour. A thread of joy and hope.

Each day we walked down to the Main Building for our lessons. The house mistress told us what was expected.

"Now, new girls. These are the rules for walking to the Main Building for your lessons each day."

"You must never wear your indoor shoes outside. Outdoor shoes only! All your shoes must be cleaned regularly."

"In the morning, you will be told which outdoor coat to wear."

We had a maroon macintosh, a tweed winter coat, and a striped blazer. All labelled.

"You are to change your shoes in the cloakroom, then put your coats on and wait for your prefect. She will check you are correctly dressed and then escort you down to the Main Building. Is that clear."

"Yes Miss Armstrong"

"Once you are familiar with the routine and route, you will be checked and allowed to walk in year groups to the Main Building."

"Yes Miss Armstrong."

Our walk, always in twos, was right out of the drive and then left down the road to the Main Building opposite Great Malvern Station. There was a rhythm to the walk, the roads crossed, to the days. I was still a small independent girl naturally happy and free but without a dog or cows. Armour still on, but changing to survive in this new place. Still confident. Prone to getting muddy. In the early years of MGC I thrived. I learnt routines quickly. Lessons were easy. I had residual resilience, and family threads still held. I was an independent girl trained to walk, to problem solve and laugh; I loved walking the Malvern Hills even in crocodiles.

"Come on, move along!"... I sang happily, slapping the boot of a stationary car which had paused before pulling out of a side road on our route. To my surprise the driver stopped and stepped out.

"What do you think you are doing? How dare you touch my car. You are a disgrace to your uniform. I could report you."

"Oh."

Miss Armstrong's deputy had more to tell us.

"After your morning lessons you will walk back here for your lunch. Then you will proceed to your allocated games session during the afternoon. These groups will be posted by the PE department on boards in your cloakroom. This will be either hockey or lacrosse."

"Remember, you must remember to look at them."

"Find your name, the group you are in, the time of your game, this will be 1.50pm, 2.20pm or 3.05pm."

"So, after your lunch you change into your games kit and proceed to your game."

"Is that clear?"

"Yes Miss Armstrong"

Maroon divided skirt, navy pants and cream shirt, cream V-neck jumper. Black canvas boots for winter and Green Flash tennis shoes for summer.

"Hockey pitches are over the road from the Main Building and the lacrosse pitches are further away. A senior girl will take you for your first week, but after that you will be expected to find your own way."

After morning lessons we gathered in the cloakroom. Found the lists.

"Susy, your name is here. Orton S. 3.05pm Lacrosse. Pitch 4a"

"I think 3.05pm is for the brainy ones who don't like games."

The basement cloakrooms were our landing place. Each House had a space. Cloakrooms were small cramped social spaces for meeting girls from other Houses before launching into or leaving each timetabled, regimented day. Outdoor clothes off and hung on a named peg. The Main Building. The heart of MGC. Corridors, six floors, stairs, many stairs, big front stairs, winding back stairs with netting to stop falling, empty classrooms, bedrooms for sixth form boarders level three and four, music practice rooms level six, girls played endless piano scales, classrooms, wood panels, everywhere wood panels and a brass bell rung by a prefect at the change of every lesson, manually. Endless. Big. Up to class or back to our houses. During the first winter, my days took a turn for the better. 1.50 games.

"Susy Orton you are quite good at games, aren't you, not like your sister."

"I think we need to switch you to 1.50pm games. You will have to have a quick lunch to get to your game on time."

I was the only one in my house to have 1.50 games so my freedom and lasting friendships began.

"Who's on 1.50 games!" I shouted as I read my name for the first time.

"I am, I am ... and I am!"

The gang was forming. We were to be close friends for the rest of our school days.

I learnt fast and thrived. Lacrosse was just joyful freedom. Running fast all over a pitch with no boundaries. I had watched the interplay of Charlton, Law and Best, at Manchester United. I loved it! Hockey. I found I was a fast runner: they put me on the wing.

"Pass it to Susy she's fast ..."

"Cross it ... cross it ... into the D ... "

"Oh no ... she's been tripped ..."

I rolled over, stood up and I kept running. That Wolfhound had taught me well. I was unfettered. Free to excel. So I did. I was one of only three girls given Under 15 'colours', awarded by MGC for the first time. I played in the first team for years, for

Worcester County Teams. Picked for territorial teams. Sport helped me survive. It also opened a door into my heart.

"Susy, as you are the best at PE in the House, we are making you the House Rounders captain. Even though you are only a third year"

"We have never won the cup so good luck. First practice on Wednesday evening."

Initial attendance and confidence were low. I thought perhaps I could change that. I was positive I could. [Sarah tells me now she is going to have a t-shirt printed with "Sue is a positive creature." I was. I am.]

Self esteem was low.

"As I'm not very good I'll go into the deep."

"I can't bowl or catch"

"We usually get beaten because other teams hit the ball into the deep field and we can't get the ball back."

I remembered my dad. Throwing to my dad had taught me to be accurate. Confident. So I suggested we practise like I had. Throwing and catching. Having fun. More girls came to practice. The better throwers taught the less confident ones. Slowly we changed.

"This is such fun. I can throw and catch now!"

The team had ideas.

"I'll go in the deep 'cos I can throw a long way and get the ball back and stop them running."

"Now I can throw and catch, perhaps I can be on one of the bases?"

We won the cup.

I loved playing sport. I was good, possibly very good.

"We have picked you to play in the hockey and lacrosse first teams even though you are still under 15."

"You have been selected to play for Worcester County Teams for hockey and lacrosse. Well done."

"Your lacrosse territorial trials have gone well, they have selected you to play for the Midlands."

"The school has decided to award you Junior Colours for both sports for the first time, ever."

I never did walk on the school stage to get my colours. An early end to my summer term for a family holiday prevented it. I had them in an envelope before stitching them proudly to my maroon pleated, uniform, regulation shorts.

Before games there was school house lunch.

Good table manners were strictly the order of the day. Meals were served at six tables. A chart with your place each week. The Head Mistress' table the most dreaded.

"Susan, pass the potatoes please."

"Sit up straight."

"Susan, what have you learnt today?"

"Susan, gather the plates and take them to the trolley."

Meals were quiet mostly. Making sure everyone had whatever they needed before you began to eat. Youngest last. Each day you moved round a place, like roulette. Subtle subservience and life training. Training for a family table in the home counties. I swallowed it. Seven days, so only two next to the Head. It was similar at every table but easing. Luckily I had my mum on my lap. Napkins. Matron: good behaviour. Assistant Matron: goodish behaviour. Head Girl: usually easy going. Other table: relaxed and with second helpings. Once my sporting ability was recognised I escaped.

"Please Miss, can I get down? I have to get to 1.50 games?"

"Yes Susan."

SPORT

My Uncle had been accepted at Oxford University in the 1930's. His rugby prowess influencing the place. He read engineering. There was something different going on in my boarding school in the 1960's: we were girls. The Football Association still banned women from playing football. Women could not run further than 800m at the Olympics. We 'played games' but they were divorced from our future aspirations. Games were not a proper subject. Girls should either be wives or, if they were academic and could remember facts, then probably spinsters. Education somehow didn't see me ... so for a long time I didn't see myself. Education separated my head from my heart and soul. But an unconscious thread of interest for facilitating teams and teamwork was there. It was to be a lifeline much later.

Then there was homophobia. Girls together were discouraged. Sport especially. There were wisps of distaste, unpleasant 'things' might go on. Nothing explicit, just dark whispered rumours. Some of my friends who were good at sport talked about PE college but rumours were rife that only lesbians went to those. My homophobia kicked in. Reinforced by my mum's best friend.

"You don't want to do PE Susy, there will be lesbians there, and you certainly don't want to be one of those."

Everywhere unspoken subtle homophobia. So I was homophobic too. It was to be my silent unconscious poisoned chalice. Later in my life, I asked Jane about crushes.

"Did you ever have crushes on girls at school?"

"Everyone had crushes on older girls and teachers, Susy. They were a normal part of Malvern."

"Oh."

"Well ... until we all got boys!"

"Oh."

I have no recollection when I sensed that loving other women might not be alright. Possibly when my friends "got boys" and I didn't. There was a girl called Maggie, older than me, dark hair, soft brown eyes. She sang in the school choir walking in ahead of the rest of us to sing at assembly. I used to daydream about her and try and get in a row so I could see her, most days.

"Susan, move along now, concentrate and walk in line with your class!"

I never told anyone, ever, but she was my compass for the day.

Family connection came at exeats. Weekend visits from my mum and dad. A tenuous thread, thinning as the years past. Mostly I remember my dad. I think my mum was sad and missed me. I don't remember her visiting. I had her napkins.

"Susy, why do you have coloured napkins when the rest of us have white linen?"

"My mum."

Memories of closeness, of home, were short and quickly snatched away. Exeats. Spitting cherry pips into the river at Upton-upon-Severn.

"Oh cherries, let's sit at the top of the steps and see if we can spit the stones into the river."

"Push with your tongue and lips ... nearly ... harder ... you need to make a noise ... Phhh!!"

"In the river!!"

I shared a love of sport with my dad.

Together. On one hot summer afternoon in 1969 on exeat, we were sitting in his car in a Worcestershire country lane. A quiet gentle dozy English summer afternoon. We were listening to the final round of The Open Golf being played in Lytham St Annes. A British player in the lead.

"There hasn't been a British winner since 1951."

"Tony Jacklin is in the lead ... can he hang on... this is exciting."

"Dad ... *dad* ... there is a bumble bee in the car ... it won't go away ..."

"Kill it."

"NO!"

"Jacklin has made a birdie!"

"... I don't want to kill it."

"I think he might do it!"

"I know ... I'll put the bee into a paper bag..."

"He's leading with only three holes to go ... "

"Dad ... the bumble bee is making a hole in the bag, eating it!"

"He's done it ... he's the Open Champion!

"Dad ... *dad* ... the bee has escaped! It's eaten its way out of the bag!"

He took me back to MM011.

That year I passed eight O levels including English Literature and Language. I had no space in myself for wondering what I wanted to do or study. No thoughts anywhere of who I was and what I might do in my life. A wife perhaps? I don't remember choosing my A levels. After my O level results my mum and dad came to MGC and had an interview with one of the teachers. It was about me, but no-one knew who I was.

"I'm afraid Sue is not university material."

I took A level History, Geography and General Studies plus homophobia and swallowing shame. Heavy on facts but barren ground for my creative imagination.

Luckily there was Oops.

SAILING: OOPS

Hayling Island. Summer holidays. Gran's house was a few doors down the road from my mum's sister Bertie where my cousin Chris lived. A short walk from my Gran's. High hedges. The pine smell of Macrocarpa still takes me there.

" Dad, can I go down to Auntie Bertie's house and see Chris?"

"... 'cos Chris wants to go sailing at Mengham Rythe Sailing Club with his new boat Oops and he wants me to go too and be his crew."

"... do you think I'll be able to remember what you taught me in Faun at Elton?"

"Yes I'm sure you and Chris will be fine, just like Bill and I were at Aldeburgh."

"That's good."

My dad had supported my cousin Chris in learning to sail and in buying a second hand Heron dinghy. Twelve foot long and four foot wide, ply-wood. Sturdy and stable. Two person beginners' boat. Perfect for two cousins to sail in Chichester Harbour. We spent that first morning exploring Oops. Putting up sails, finding out how everything worked. My dad who could do lettering from when he was an architect had painted Oops on her stern with MRSC next to it. We loved her already.

"Are we going to race?"

Chris had heard my dad's stories too.

"Yea ... I think we can. There's a race for small dinghies called the Slow Handicap."

"Will there be a course?"

"Yea, round buoys in the harbour."

We had seen the harbour chart on the club house wall. Lots of different marks in the harbour. Complicated.

"I've an idea, why don't we get one of those small plastic maps of Chichester Harbour, I've seen them on other boats, we can stick it on the deck and see the buoys."

"Good idea."

Saturday morning. Our first race. We signed our names on the race sheet.

"Why don't you go and find out the course ... it will be on the clubhouse board."

"Ok ... I'll write it on my arm so I can read it when we are sailing."

"Good. We can see the marks on the chart too."

"Let's get ready early and into the water before the start time so we can work out where the start line is and which tack we will need to be on."

"OK. I'll take the trolley up the slipway and bring her head to wind to get the sails up."

"Great. Ok ready to go... push her off ... "

A shout from the shore ...

"Are you two wearing lifejackets?"

"Yes Auntie Bertie."

"You will take care now and don't do anything foolish."

"No Auntie Bertie."

"I'll wait here in the club house until you are home safe."

"We will be fine, Auntie Bertie honestly. You don't need to wait. The race could take a long time as we don't go very fast, and the wind might drop."

"I shall be here dear, waiting until I see you safe."

"Yes Auntie Bertie." we chorused.

Chris mouthed "Let's get out of here and find that start line."

"Have you found the course?"

"Yep, on the back of my hand. Club line, Black Can to port, Double Cross to port, Channel to starboard, that could be a gybe ... South West Pilsey to starboard, Stocker to port then home via Double Cross and the Black Can to the line."

"Right, look out for our class flag, I think it's the red, white and blue pennant. When that goes up with the hooter, we have five minutes to the start."

We were in our element. Racing ... perfecting our tacking and gybing ...

"Ready about ... lee oh"

A few hours later, wet, happy and tired we sailed up the channel with the wind dropping on the last of the falling tide, mud appearing, past the Black Can and towards the finishing line."

"I think the hooter will go to signal we have finished."

"I think we may be the last to finish. I wonder where we have come?"

"Oh no your mum is still on the slipway!"

As we dropped the sails and pulled Oops up the slipway the race officer called out ...

"Well done you two, last in but you have just won the race."

"Wow, that's great. How have we done that?"

"Your little Heron has a good handicap. Once we worked out yours with your time, you were first."

"That's fantastic ... When's the next race?"

This is how we spent our summers. Often at Mengham but if we were lucky we were towed to regattas at other clubs in the harbour. My fear of bangs sometimes frightened me.

"Is that a gunshot ... ?"

"Yes for regattas they start the races with a shotgun not a hooter."

"Oh ... "

"I think the start line is close to the club house, and in this wind we will need to be close up to windward of the line to get a good start like your dad taught me."

"Oh ... "

"Why have you put your fingers in your ears? Hold the jib sheet in!"

"Sorry, I don't like guns."

Despite my fears, I loved every minute of our summer sailing. We won several cups. Shredded the nerves of Auntie Bertie and learnt how to sail our beloved Oops all over the harbour in all weathers. My apprenticeship for a lifetime of sailing.

SIXTH FORM

So six form. Much more freedom and boys. Boys at nearby Malvern College. Boys. Most of my friends 'got' boys. I tried. I wrote to a boy at another public school I had met at home. He wrote back. I went to parties and snogged boys. But it didn't seem to work for me. No electricity. I couldn't stop the heart wrenching, deep seated passionate feeling I had looking at women, but not with boys. I didn't dare even think or acknowledge it let alone talk about it.

Sixth form started well enough. I was moving from MMO11 into the Main Building hopefully with three friends.

"We have put you in a dorm with your three first choices." Janie, Jane and Vanessa.

"That's great."

"You are next door to Miss McGregor, the residential sixth form tutor."

"Oh, thank you."

Living in the Main Building. Many floors, many corridors, many stairs. Lower sixth. Dormitory of four friends. Level 3 or 4. Laughter and mischief. A very amateur theatre production during a national power cut. Candles! Fun and games. Senior colours, beating arch lacrosse rivals Westonbirt. My straight, confident, happy boarding school girl was forming. Staying alert. Coping. Confident. Capable. A wonderful disguise.

"I bet you can't throw a shoe out of the window from here?"

"I bet I can ... if I throw it sideways it will fit through ... wow ... I've done it! ... it's on the staffroom roof!"

"Shh you two ... or Gregs will hear us ... "

We lived in a huge retired victorian hotel with six floors, and stairs. Many stairs.

"Now girls, you may use all the staircases in the building except the main staircase by the front door and the Headmistresses Office. That is out of bounds"

Not for long.

"I bet she's not in her office in the evening."

Mischief continued.

"What are you two doing here at two o'clock in the morning?"

"Watching the World Cup football in Mexico. We've turned the sound down!"

"I see. What *am* I to do with you two, and one of you a prefect?"

Silent hopeful smiles ...

"Well ... If only you had put something under the door, I wouldn't have seen the light."

"How long does it go on ... it's after half time Miss ... Alright then watch the match finish and go back to your rooms quietly!"

"Phew ... "

Sport played a central part in my life especially in the winter. We were a happy gang playing hockey and lacrosse every afternoon. Empty after the younger girls had walked back to their houses. We had the run of the place. We were trusted. Left to our own devices. Implicit messages that we were special, privileged... Malvern Girls were entitled, capable and the top of the pile.

We walked everywhere.

"Let's meet at the back gate and walk down to lacrosse ... "

Our walk there and back is something I remember very clearly. My last walk there on a damp March day at the end of my last spring term broke my heart.

"Do you think we will ever meet like this again?"

"No, we leave in the summer so we won't play lacrosse together again."

Over the fields and down a muddy path with brambles and hawthorn, steep, slippery. The small battered wooden pavilion central to the pitches. I spent many happy hours there.

In my first term there was one woman who was a sixth form tutor and games teacher. I couldn't get her out of my mind. I would hope for glimpses of her. Linger on the back stairs hoping to see her as she returned to her room. Accidentally bump into her. Offer to run errands.

"Do you know what happened to Liz, she went to PE college didn't she? Yes, she went to live with that game's mistress you liked."

"Oh. That would explain why she was always in her room."

Absurd now as I write it, but there it was. I was terrified someone might see me waiting. See inside my head. Hear my heartbeat. See a tattoo on my chest saying 'lesbian' and know. I silently hated myself. I really hated myself. Why didn't I stop and pull myself together? Main Building is empty in the evenings and week-ends. Good for wandering. Good for illicit music listening. I discovered that the main hall had a turntable and speakers on stage. I played Jacques Loussier Trio - Bach endlessly. Hopelessly. Afraid.

"Stay silent. Stay straight. Ignore who you are. If you follow the straight path, perhaps get married, it will go away. Please, please it will go away."

"It's time for the school picture everyone! The chairs are on the front lawn. Two o'clock after lunch. Blazers for prefects, blouses with ties everyone else, and ... clean shoes. Don't be late."

"Prefects will be on the chairs with the staff. Head girl and deputy next to the tutors. The other prefects next to them."

"Hurry along now the photographer isn't staying all day!"
"Do you think they will run round?"
"Yep sure of it."
"Remember everyone, the camera will sweep along the rows so stay very still. And SMILE!"

I'm sitting there in a striped blazer, a prefect. Hair tied back. Blue blouse, tie, heather tweed skirt, tights and slip on leather shoes. One of the selected few seated on the front row with tutors. Silently. Smiling at the camera. Other friends, long lost, were ranged around us. It is our A level summer. Exams.

My group of friends didn't see much of each other because we were supposed to be revising for exams in our rooms.

"I need those 3'B's to get into University. I want to read Law."

But I wasn't. I was sitting in a brown wood panelled room staring at huge lever arch files full of facts about history, geography and general studies. With my mind elsewhere.

Dreaming. In love with a girl. Ashamed of myself. Silent. Terrified.

JUNE DAYS

"I'll meet you by the big old oak at the top of the tennis field at 4.30 OK?"

"Bring your revision stuff and we can test each other on the History notes."

Sitting with her under a big tree on the top playing field, with tennis courts and rounders pitches. Leafy and full, full summer. Sensing it was wrong, not really reciprocated, yet loving that captivating joy of being together. I gathered illicit down like a nesting bird. Blind to what came next. She would leave and get married. I probably would too. But then. High summer. Grass cut intoxication. Heady heartfelt bliss. Yet at the edge of horror, just round the corner. Endlessly, hopelessly blind to anything else. An island, settled, smooth and all embracing. The structure of a false dawn that I couldn't possibly imagine. Certainly no study. Blissful ignorance. Perhaps. A quiet gentle ride before rapids and destruction. That summer there was no-one else. Just the two of us. Warm, beautiful in the final weeks of my settled time. It's so painful to write now. Like those movies of croquet and village cricket before the First World War. All boaters and cocktails, all light and fluffy before the mud and hell.

I used to dream of this time. Green lawns in summer with big blousy trees and I'm still on my knees weeping, stripped and alone, torn limb from heart with labels redundant. A last trunk waiting to be packed. Never quite packed. Joy, happiness and hope were not on the list anymore, just closets, failure and loneliness.

Such a contrast to optimistic thirteen year old me skipping happily down to 1.50 games. But that was it, the trap.

When I left school I split myself into two. Unconscious then. I tore out my creative heart. I dug a deep deep hole on the gentle sunny slopes of my last summer love, buried my joy and walked away. Desperate. Tears. Distress. Silent. I was about to be launched into the most difficult, lonely years of my life. Secure here with this school family was to be my last experience of safety for a long time. No wonder I didn't get very good grades for my A levels. I wasn't university material.

SKIN THREAD - SHAME

In August 2018 I watched Nanette, Hannah Gadsby's award winning stand up routine in which she, a lesbian, gets very personal about what it's like being a lesbian. She is angry, very angry. I have a visceral response. Shifting.

"If you soak a child in shame, they cannot develop neurological pathways that carry thought. Especially thoughts of self worth." Hannah Gadsby - 'Nanette'.

"Have you found a boyfriend? I'm sure Mr Right will come along soon."

"oh yes ... I keep looking."

Bloody hell.

HEALTH WARNING

My memories then are painful. Difficult. Fragmented. Many pieces only recently unearthed, dusted off and valued in therapy. A jumble. Happy and secure with friends, yet silent to myself and to close friends, of my true desires. I have one close, dear school friend from this time ...

"But Susy, we never even thought to talk about sexuality, it just wasn't there. I think we all swallowed homophobia."

I was stumbling, smiling, marrying, lying, hurting, denying, scared. Silent. Split. Yes there are creative threads of me there, patches of happiness and enjoyment, I had to live a life. But not my life. Not my true life. Because you see I am and was not in charge of the world and its opinions. It's rampant, poisonous homophobia. I was barely in charge of my own life then. I hid myself well. Swallowing trauma renders people rudderless, devious, wary, uncertain, watchful, nervous of detection, not strong, grounded or certain. I was all of these. Duplicitous.

I now know that my body was holding on until I was really truly safe. Safe, loved, treasured. Only then was I ready to turn, to dig deep, and to face myself, so my skin could let go. But it wasn't ok. It was excruciating,

And there was more disturbance to come.

HOME

After I left school I went home. I went home but it wasn't home. Everything had changed. My family was looking the other way. Preoccupied. Seemingly indifferent.

Susy, finished school, job done.

But it wasn't home anymore. It was a big house in Bury that I had not lived in for years. It was the same but different. I could slide on the hall rugs. My mirror was there on the cloakroom wall, at shoulder height. The lawn, the flowerbeds where I stopped boundaries and played catch with my dad, but no Tarka. The beech hedge. Raspberry patch where I lost Dindy, bare now from marital decay. Where was everyone? Gone back south like homing pigeons. They never liked the north. Jane was in London and didn't come home very often.

"Can I bring Frank home for the weekend?"

Their car drew into Garsdale drive. Evening. Dim light.

"Hi mum this is Frank. He works with me at the Adventure Playground. He's studying politics."

Out of the car stepped a very tall, very black man.

"Really good to meet you Mr Orton and Mrs Orton."

"... er yes it's good to meet you."

It was an interesting weekend. Later I discovered my parents were silently brewing a divorce. The dinner table was strained. My mother was menopausal and threatened with a hysterectomy. The 1970's solution to painful women's 'issues', take them out. My father was courting his secretary. Blatantly. Inviting her to 'drinks' in our sitting room with office colleagues at Christmas. I was different too. I was full of shame. Hiding. Working hard not to be myself. Nervous of betraying myself. I had learnt to watch. Not to attract attention or disagree. I pretended I was ok. I was probably sad and lonely but couldn't find it, couldn't acknowledge it.

I became one of those happy capable boarding school girls, independent, carefree, able to cope anywhere. Serve drinks, smile at my parents' friends, and put up with their roaming hands on my bottom. I was heterosexual, and in search of a husband to fulfil my proper life. I was good. I fooled my family. I convinced myself. I thought it was the only route.

Women's choices in 1970's were limited: teacher, secretary or nurse. I spent a term in a secretarial college in Oxford but was thrown out for laughing in shorthand tests and playing lacrosse for the university. Unsure what to do with myself I worked in a care home to raise money to go to the USA on a Greyhound bus trip. I had to go with a family 'boy friend' who I didn't like.

"It wouldn't be safe for you to go on your own, Susy."

In New York we tried hamburgers and heard police sirens. He tried to get into bed with me in one downtown hotel somewhere in Montana but I told him to get lost.

I met some business friends of my dad. The Werlys. They had a big house in Connecticut. A pool. I ate my first McDonalds. They were kind and generous. Glen gave me a silver dollar. Lost now in all my moving. They saw me and I felt it. Asked about me. Cared about me. It felt like the family I didn't have.

"Into the pool everyone. Five lengths and last out gets the breakfast!"

"OK you guys today is a fun day, a holiday, get yourselves a drink and and a burger and we're settling in for the Super Bowl"

"No, not over there, all on the sofas so we get a good view."

"Do you guys know the rules ? ... it's a bit like your rugby."

I had not had so much fun in years. Fran held me in a long hug before they took us to the bus station. Heading west.

"You take care now. Come and see us anytime you can."

In America? I cried on the bus when we left, not knowing why. My watch was stolen in a washroom in Chicago. I watched sea otters cradling their babies in the water while sleeping on a deck overlooking the Pacific at Big Sur. Hours and hours on Greyhound buses. Rodeo. Galveston, because of Glen Campbell. He wasn't there.

Then back to Bury and indecision. Another job in a care home? A levels not good enough for University. I wasn't university material. What now?

I could have said "I'm not OK."
I could have said "I'm sad."
I could have said "I'm lonely."
I could have said "I'm struggling."
I could have said "I'm frightened."
I could have said "I'm terrified of what comes next."
I could have said "I'm very very scared of who I am."
I could have said "I'm on the outside, looking in."
I could have said "I think I'm different."
I could have said "Please, hug me."
I could have said "Why aren't you like the Werly's."
I could have said ...
... but I didn't. I stayed silent and swallowed it all down. Just like school had taught me.

PE was all I knew I was good at. But I badly didn't want to be a teacher. I loved the idea of understanding people and differences. Groups and teams. Anthropology appealed. The family messages were clear.

Auntie B: "You don't want to do anthropology Susy, it's all about natives in foreign places and you don't want any of that. Teaching is safe and reliable."

"Your A levels are not good enough for university."

"Teaching?"

"All your aunts and cousins teach."

"You need to do something to support yourself until you get married."

"You are good at sport, perhaps PE college?"

COLLEGE

I was malleable. I had to be. The best PE college which offered lacrosse and hockey was in Liverpool. It was single sex and had a reputation for lesbians.

"You don't want to do PE Susy because there are lesbians and you don't want to be one of those."

Not there then. I didn't really want to be a teacher. All my mother's family were teachers. So I applied for a second rate PE college in Chichester which didn't offer lacrosse, my favourite sport which I was very good at. Why Chichester? I'm not sure I was brave enough to strike out on my own then, so stayed close to the 'family' home. A mistake. My lacrosse stick was in a wardrobe in my mum's house for years before she threw it away. Lacrosse stick making is now an extinct craft.

My eldest cousin, sister of my sailing buddy Chris, was bossy, she lived nearby.

"You can't go to your interview in trousers."

"Why not?"

"It's not suitable."

Acquiescence.

"Here, you can wear my woollen skirt suit."

Really that's awful!

"How am I supposed to do anything practical in that ...? "

"Don't be silly, Susy this is much more acceptable."

Forward rolls were difficult but I was accepted in my wool suit.

I moved into halls of residence in Chichester.

"During the first year of your Physical Education course you need to choose which group you want to be in."

"Either the games group, who will concentrate more on outdoor team activities, or the dance group who will do more gymnastics and dance."

I looked at my fellow students. Games group. Short hair, butch. Dance group feminine, straight. I loved games from school. Too risky for my denial.

"I'll join dance."

"First years, in the dance studio, leotards, ready to warm up at 9 am."

Our dance lecturer was tall, very long legs. Not someone to partner with for leg stretch pairs exercises sitting down. There was always an undignified rush to find another partner.

"Ah Sue. With me."

"Sitting forward bends with legs apart, feet flexed soles together opposite your partner."

"Now ease your head to the floor between your legs. Letting your partner help you."

Just the thought brings tears to my eyes. My short hamstrings are not made to stretch like that!

Jane appeared to be flourishing. She was working in an adventure playground in Notting Hill Gate. And she had a dog. Beauty. Gentle soft, wolf-like creature who followed her close at heel without a lead, on busy London streets. I went to see her in London. She helped me along. Full of good ideas.

"Would you like to have your eyelashes dyed Susy? Saves on mascara and is great for sailing."

"Yes."

My first eyelash tint at Joan Price's Face Place.

"Gin and tonic is good when you have 'the curse' Susy."

"We'll go to Kensington market too, it's great for loons and afghan jackets."

While sailing in Hayling Island she had met a friendly tall Royal Navy officer, who drove a Triumph sports car. I think it was serious because he drove 200 miles north to Garsdale to see her. She became thinner having her wisdom teeth out.

I, meanwhile, was wondering what I was doing with my life. I worked hard on my disguise. I made big efforts to be girly and flirt with the boys. To add to my disguise I was openly homophobic. At college several women wore very masculine clothes, had very short hair, no make up. They were all good at games. I was frightened of their look. They often went on weekend trips to Bournemouth which had the reputation of being a closet gay town. I joined in the taunts.

"Did you have a nice time in Bournemouth?" parodied with a very camp accent.

At the end of my first year I had a boyfriend. We went hitch-hiking in Europe. He had a lime green Cortina and lived in Gosport. We camped on a hill overlooking Florence. It was beautiful. Our tiny tent uncomfortable. Germans eating salami and cheese for breakfast. In the market I had found and bargained for a chess set for Jane as a wedding present. Leather, hand carved pieces. It was beautiful. Pausing on an evening walk over the Ponte Vecchio, I started to cry.

"What are you crying about? You are here on holiday in this beautiful city. And I care for you so much."

"I'm sorry, I don't know."

I couldn't stop. I was unconsolable. Wretched.

In 2017 I saw the film 'Carol' all about a passionate lesbian love affair. Oscar nominated, beautifully staged with a jazz music soundtrack. It had a big impact on me. I saw myself.

A film journalist observed:

"Sitting watching Carol, I saw two women watching the film sitting in front of me with arms around each other engrossed in the plot. I realised then that for all of my life I had been seeing representations of myself on screens, in films. I realised too that watching Carol, was for these women, really groundbreaking; a beautifully portrayed film with top actors portraying a happy lesbian love story."

My journal records my reaction.

First day alive | Carol
Something has shifted, scars from my soul, unshackled, released, floating free, washes of deep emotion, close to tears of joy, of relief, of sadness long held. It's as if I had no idea what was missing deep inside until today. Today is an ordinary extraordinary December day. Welling up in soft enveloping pulses, swamps of stuff releases ... Releases, yes releases me to be me in the world, proud, feet placed firmly, each toe down.

SEPARATION

Home to Manchester Piccadilly train station with the chess set wrapped in my rucksack amongst my dirty t-shirts and grubby towel.

"Can you pick me up from Manchester Piccadilly station after my holiday with Pete? He's going home to Cosham?"

"Your father and I will pick you up."

My mum never said 'father' unless there was something wrong. Like calling me Susan if they were cross with me.

"Why are you both here?"

"Just get in the back of the car Susy. Your father and I have something to tell you."

Backed out of the parking space. Traffic lights. Roundabouts. Manchester Road to Bury.

My mother turned around in the passenger seat of my dad's company car. A Rover 2000 pale blue with leather seats.

"We are separating."

"Oh."

"Your mother will be moving out."

"I shall stay here because of my work."

"Oh."

I don't remember arriving home. I don't remember much of the next few months. My family continued to get on with their lives around me. Jane's wedding. Idyllic Bosham Church. Awful bridesmaids dress.

"Jane is getting married in Bosham Church near Chichester and afterwards at Stonewalls."

"Not from home?"

"No."

"You will be one of her bridesmaids."

"What will I have to wear?"

"Your dress will be long empire style in a lovely blue flowery print. Your cousin is making the dresses."

"Will I have to wear heels?"

"Yes. Blue sandals."

"After they are married, where will they live, dad?"

"I have helped them with a deposit for a cottage at Langstone."

"Your mother is also giving Jane her three year old mini traveller."

"The green one?"

To this day I have difficulty putting days and dates in any order. Sequentially. Difficult. I must have unpacked my treasured chess set. I gave it to Jane. I think she may still have it.

THEN WHAT

I think my mum was devastated by the separation. Hysterectomy. Menopause. Stripped of her role as JP. She moved back 'home' south where her sisters were. Depressed. Alone. Without income. My father moved in with his mistress. Garsdale, home, felt lost to me.

Much later, repeatedly my mother would say to me.

"I told your father that you would come off worse if we separated."

"He said, Susy will be fine, she's independent, she's eighteen. I had to cope when I was nine ... "

My repeated reply.

"I'm ok mum."

Looking back I wonder where I was with myself. Lonely. Unsure. Hiding it well. I attempted to stay in touch with both my parents.

Drawn to support my mum in her distress. Driving to Havant after college classes and leaving late.

"Don't worry I always have enough sleeping pills by my bed."

Staying with my dad.

"Ethne is cooking supper at her place. So we won't be at Garsdale."

Most of me was at college in a daze, working hard, playing, having boyfriends, dancing at college to Hi Ho Silver Lining at the disco after finishing an essay. I joined in the drinking at the college local pub. Got pissed on vodka. Can't touch it now.

Recently I was sitting on the playing fields of Chichester recreation ground, opposite the college grounds. With my nieces and nephew and partners, children playing happily. I remembered how sad and unhappy I was there in the 1970's and said so.

"But Susy, surely not, you have always been such a happy person."

I was a good liar, good actor. Very skilled at denial.

The final years at college were punctuated with disguise

"Have you found a bloke for the end of year dinner?"

"No but I'll find one ..."

My exam results were ok but not enough to qualify for the degree year with my friends.

"We are disappointed Sue, you certainly are capable but it's your dissertation that's let you down. All that moving and travelling in the holidays to your parents ..."

Not University material.

CATHERINE

"Jenny, while you rest I'll come up and breast feed Catherine. A chat always helps me relax."

My mum pregnant with me and her best friend Barbara. Separated by our move north but inseparable. A lifelong link. My sisters godmother.

I have known Catherine all my life. Lucky me.

Every summer holiday from Hayling we had picnics on the South Downs. Tea and parties at their house Stonewalls was a treat. Holding the 'home' thread tight as Bury wasn't. Our families connected.

We were not 'best friend' close but I've always felt her support even through my denial. She is close from a distance. Watching, embracing me with care.

So often in my life, Catherine has sought me out, travelled, looked me in the eyes, asked, listened, and seen me. Seen through my defences perhaps. Sitting in my small cramped room in college in the 1970's. She asked me how I was. I probably said

"I'm fine." But I think she sensed I wasn't.

Catherine is a warm and constant thread and you will find her woven into this story like fine silk.

REFLECTIONS

Today I'm quite an ordered happy soul. I remember things. Where I put that summer blanket for picnics. Where my keys are. Usually. I enjoy my life. I have choices. My love of rice and gravy. A throwback to childhood mealtimes. Roast lamb, vegetables. Fish and chips. Pickled onions and cheddar cheese. Sailing on the breeze. Walking the downs. Sarah. Gorgeous. So now, as I look back to those years, I wonder how I managed to stay hidden for so long. After boarding school and parental separation. I split. Denial. Forgot my self for years.

As I write I can see more clearly. I was different. I behaved the same but I was different. Hiding a dark secret. How did I do that? How clear can we be of our early adult sensibilities? I found a picture of myself in a Laura Ashley dress, calf length, floaty. I'm posing on Garsdale rockery, lounging on a low wall one knee bent showing my calf, with slingback blue sandals with a block heel. Around my neck is a pink scarf, carelessly wrapped. A straw wide brimmed hat completes my effortless fabrication. Was that me? Looking at it now I feel as though there is a mist of insecurity and longing tucked in somewhere. What colour is shame? What was this persona I would perfect for years. Adrianne Rich calls it a retreat into sameness. Heterosexuality was the norm, so being and acting the same is safer.

"Sameness is the most passive and debilitating of responses to political repression, economic insecurity, and a renewed open season on difference."

These layers, this protection, this skin, were to hide me from myself and my family for years.

PATTERNS

Now I see that my behaviour in response to my circumstances was complex. Many layers. Unconscious for such a long time. Separation. Layers. Garsdale was down a mile long lane separated from any community. I had friends at a primary school but not nearby. Then at eleven boarding school separated me from them, from my parents and from Jane. Closeness and familiarity didn't happen. Except 200 miles away at MMO11.

"Did you go to Brownies and Guides?"

"No, I was not at home long enough. MGC didn't do Guides."

"Did you have a gang building a bonfire in November?"

"No, I was away at school."

This is not about the loss of a rose-tinted adolescence. I am sure I would have been pushing boundaries, having arguments and fallings out. But I would have been with them. Growing up in sight. In plain sight. But instead isolation, separation. My family was not a safe space for me. We didn't know each other. Then there was my separation from myself. That is much more difficult. Would I have told anyone? I doubt it. Someone might have noticed my growing unease. Especially my artist mum. I'm sure she would have been supportive. Later she was.

"If only I had been in a better place when your father and I separated, I might have noticed your unhappiness and I would have told you your sexuality was just fine." 2010

My disguise was flawless. If you had met me in a sailing club or pub then I would have been as homophobic as the next person. More so probably. But the seismic rumblings of denial were with me all my life. I met a doctor once, an anthroposophical doctor. He suggested:

"We walk backwards into our future and as we do we see our lives spreading out in front of us."

Looking back now I can see my phases of denial. To marriage. Ten years.

"If I get married 'it' will go away."

But I know this feisty girl was always there. Breathing from the depths. She is there. She's me. I denied her. She was coated in the green slime of homophobia and loss. But she was there. At the core of it all was me. My loved centre. Thank goodness. Waiting, gathering strength.

"I was a small person, balanced on my feet, secure running. I was born loved and wanted; my mum told me. I liked to explore ... I would float at the top and then hold my breath and swim underwater down to the bottom and come back up. Pulling myself up each step until I bobbed to the surface and I could stand on the top step. Time and again."

"I was an independent girl, naturally happy and free. Still in grey armour. Still confident. Prone to getting muddy. I learnt routines quickly. Lessons were easy. I had residual resilience. I was an independent girl trained to walk, to problem solve and laugh. I learnt fast and thrived."

"I rolled over, stood up and I kept running. That Wolfhound had taught me well. I was unfettered. Free to excel. So I did. Until ... Sport helped me survive. It also opened a door into my heart."

She's here now. I'm here, older but free, happy and joyful. How did that happen?

THREADS AND LAYERS

I also wonder about what my body did with these experiences. I'm a physical creature. Tactile. Sensitive. My ears get cold first in the wind. Hats are important. Woollen ones. Security and warmth. My intuition too is highly developed. I sense things early. Often very early. Now post shedding I wonder at the thin layers. Laid in and down. Gossamer layer on layer down. Year on year. Silently like snow in the night. Rings round a tree. Disappointment, denial, joy, each recorded. Packed in tight to hide my heart.

THERAPY NOTES

Journal 2020
"It sounds to me as if you betrayed your creative self at Malvern."
Conforming.

Later I discovered I could write and create, especially poetry. It was the first writing I had confidence to try. I wrote a short haiku poem about my dad after he had died in 1990. Jane liked it and wondered.

"Why didn't you read English at university Susy?"

Mmmmm ... you may well ask.

I remained silent. For far too long.

After college I secured a job working in London. A 2000 girls comprehensive. I rented a room with a crate for the bedside table in Chiswick from a couple of people I knew from college. My room was small, south facing. First on the right up the stairs to the small first floor flat. Hot in the sun. I was lodging, I use the word carefully because I was not sharing. I had a feeling the two women I was lodging with were lesbians. We didn't say. I wasn't. I was so sure then. So frightened. They were friendly. I remember thinking what shapeless colourless clothes they wore. Mens shoes and haircuts. But I wasn't one of them. I was just checking. Holding myself up to see. There was no one I could talk to then. I would sit on my small single bed tired after teaching. Solitary and silent. Attempting to plan netball and gym lessons for school. I never liked it. I didn't eat much then, I have no memory of cooking.

"We are having a party on Saturday. Having a few friends round. Why don't you join us?

"Alright ... thanks."

Some evenings I would ride my Honda 70 around London streets trying to find my way around. Like a learner taxi driver. I drove north to the river, Elephant and Castle, Waterloo, north to Highgate and Kings Cross. Endless. A bit sad and lost.

My PE department gathered each day on a round window seat in the staff room. An island building overlooking the huge campus. I wore a pair of ski-pants, red stretchy with flares for my non-existent boots. Polo shirt, white or pale blue. And a top. I don't remember what colour or shape. I just turned up every day and tried. No joy. Just 3B at 9 am every Monday morning. Again and again. Then home to my room.

Then, that party.

"Everyone should be here by about 7.00 o'clock so come up when you like."

There were three steps from my single room up to the rest of the flat. I didn't often go up those steps. I'm breathing in rapidly now as I write. Thinking back to my trepidation. Like a cliff edge. Needing to look, to jump, to see. Shivering. I think there was a bathroom, 'their' bedroom and lounge, they called it lounge not sitting room. A kitchen.

"OK I'm coming."

"Come in Sue and meet everyone."

I walked in and stopped. I looked around. Paused. Took a deep breath, my stomach turning, sweaty, scared. I stepped in. The room was full of smiling short haired women dressed in tweeds and brogues sitting all round the room. Silent dread took hold ...

"... these women all look like men, oh no, fuck, they think I might be a lesbian ... I'm definitely not one of those. Definitely. Definitely. I better move out fast."

"Anyone have a room I could rent?"

"I thought you had a nice room in Chiswick with those girls from your college."

"They weren't my friends."

"I've an attic room you can have."

I left within the months notice. Moved swiftly, to a fusty attic room in a shared house in Love Lane. Straight. Three of us, all teachers. Perfect. The lid went onto my closet and was nailed firmly down. For years. It was twenty years before I shared this experience. I did learn a great recipe for spaghetti bolognaise at Love Lane. Aromas of basil, bayleaves, tomatoes simmering gently wafted into my attic. Later I moved into a shared house with Catherine and friends in Clapham South. Still I was hiding, but I was safe. I think Catherine knew I was unhappy.

"I don't know how you managed with your mother ringing you up in distress late at night."

Watching scary midnight movies helped. I was often behind the sofa.

At school I had discovered my love of the underdog, the educational misfit. I was a misfit. A silent one. How people flourish with kindness and with care. I learnt that first with my rounders team. It was a thread I would follow.

Teaching was a treadmill. Exhausting. I was disillusioned about what I was doing. Keeping children fit? Finding olympic champions? Passing exams? Certainly not being myself. Margaret Thatcher was brewing Clause 28 too, so I was wary.

I did try sailing. I would, wouldn't I? Offered to crew in races on Saturdays on an icy Thames at Putney in small dinghy with a thin, strait-laced, public school banker who never smiled. It was freezing cold. No preamble.

"I'll meet you on the slip way at mid-day prompt. That way we have ample time to rig and ready the boat onto the slip-way ready for a prompt start at thirteen hundred."

"Ok."

"Wear plenty of warm togs it can be jolly cold on the Thames."

"Ok."

Should I write the course on my hand? Probably not. As we drifted silently on the tide to the Harrods Depository blowing on my hands to stop them freezing, I dreamed of sunny summer days in Oops racing round Chichester Harbour.

"I say ... would you care to come to a rugby match at Twickers? The Varsity. Next Saturday? It will be joy good fun. All the chaps will be there, we can meet in the bar."

I do love rugby, but it didn't last.

One of my best teaching moments had been persuading the school to let me take a class of 'difficult' but talented fifth years on a trip to Crystal Palace National Sports Centre. They had been a bit of a challenge. Many of them, taller than me!

"Netball today ... why aren't you all changed?"

"We're not wearing that blooming kit ... it's freezing out there and those short skirts are awful ... "

I had to agree. Negotiations proceeded. The regulation kit was so inappropriate for the larger adolescent girl.

"How about tracksuits?"

"Too right Miss ... that would be great."

Perfect, I little rule bending on my part because tracksuits were not allowed for PE, but a result.

They loved their netball.

The head mistress had said:

"You can't possibly take them out, they will trash the place."

"I can vouch for them. They are really keen to go and know they have to behave."

We went. They loved it.

"Hey Miss, would it be ok if we went and thanked the centre manager before we leave, it's been great. When can we go again?"

Much later I qualified in humanistic education. They told me I was a gifted innovative creative facilitator. I *am* a gifted creative facilitator! But then, I didn't believe it. Not for 20 years. Still it's hard to write. I moved on. Found another job. In 2018 I discovered that the shame deep inside me prevented my flourishing, in case I revealed who and what I really was. So I moved on. I had to move on many times before I understood why.

ATLANTIC SAILING

After three years I left teaching. Unhappy. No plan. I answered an ad in Yachting Monthly to join a crew of a 42 ft ketch sailing to the West Indies. My application included:

"I have sailed since I was a child and my scrambled eggs are amazing."

They took me on.

Falmouth in December. Storm bound we stayed in the harbour. We enjoyed watching a resident friendly dolphin. A working diver had other ideas ...

"Will someone please do something about this bloody dolphin, it thinks I'm a playmate and I'm trying to fix this chain!"

My dad visited with his mistress. Awkward.

I wanted to say, "You bastard splitting up the family when I had not even left. I hate what you have done to mum and I don't want your new woman here."

Instead I said, "It's good of you to come and see me off, thank you."

He gave me a Great World Atlas. Written inside.

"To Sue Christmas 1981,

If the charts are lost, this might help.

with love, Dad and Ethne."

I have since crossed out Ethne.

Rough weather eased slightly after a week. We set sail south. Bay of Biscay. Big dark seas. Alone on watch. Fours hours on, four hours off. Cooking. Clearing up. Clipped on. Cold. Climbing each wave, surfing down the sides, sometimes leaping off them. With disastrous consequences.

"What the fuck ... the locker's have split down here and there are tins everywhere!"

Scary. Exhilarating.

"That's the entrance to Vigo on the bow. Portugal. Biscay done."

"Well done everyone, we'll go in there. We are just in time for Christmas."

Just four of us. A wild Scotsman, a couple sleeping in the aft cabin and me. Vigo.

After a three day rest and celebration. We set off. Off Lisbon, we hit heavy weather again and broke the self steering gear.

"The fucking self steering vane is not working properly. We'll have to steer all watch."

A tired crew dug deep. Into port to fix it.

"A couple of days should do it and then we can get going."

"Isn't it getting late for our crossing to the Canaries?"

More sea. More long nights at the helm. Frightened. Into Southern Portugal. Stop. Eat and drink. Boat not fit for purpose so we stopped. Stayed a while waiting and eating in Portugal. Eventually, we abandoned the trip and the scrambled eggs. They were good. Home. Stayed with mum. Needed a job. I wandered over to the local Holiday Inn and asked.

"Can you serve drinks and do bar work?

"Yea"

"Well we need someone to run The Mast Bar."

It was handy for Langstone Sailing Club where I kept Columbus.

Susy used to come and rig me between shifts. I was always waiting. Solo 1492. Her first sailing dinghy. She loved me. Gazing at the tide and wind around me. She liked a force SW 2-3 on a rising tide. Was it that today? I hoped so. If it was, I could be rigged easily and left with my bow on the slipway while she put my trolley away, before we went out.

"Ah look, the wind is right. She's decided, we are going out."

There she was. Walking over the bridge from her bar job at the Holiday Inn. Alone. No hangers on. My heart lifted.

I wondered what had brought her here. I think she was staying with her mum after a long distance sailing trip. She was between jobs. Reflective. Always sunny but deep in thought. Searching.

Her smile, lightness of step. She's taking me sailing! Cover off, sail rigged but not up. Check and tighten my beautiful full sail and wood battens, check, I had my rudder and tiller, of course. Pull me over the road and down the slipway. Head to wind on the trolley. Free my mainsheet. Sail up. Into the water. Push me off. Hang onto the painter. Trolley up the slipway, secure. Push off. Jump in. Breathe out. Sheet in. Lean out. Fly. Free. *Easy.*

I loved those sails from Langstone in the early 1980's. A gentle breeze on my bow. Susy barely touched my tiller. Light. Relaxed. Sail sheeted in just enough to fly and lean. I often wondered how she was. Quiet, reflective. No great heaving and sweating on sheets to go faster. Just relaxed. We both relaxed knowing we were together free. She soon settled into the slap slap rhythm of my bow wave. Down to the Black Can, past the withies to the top of Emsworth creek. I watched her easing, her lengthening breaths, her smile, her joy, her expertise. Her oasis perhaps. I think sailing was in her blood. But I wondered how she was. Always watchful and quiet. I wondered where she had learnt her sailing. She is so balanced and easy with me.

Perhaps in Mengham, near where we are sailing today. Past Marker and down to Channel just off Hayling Island Sailing Club. We don't often get there on a tide. Susy learnt early to be gentle in a boat. I like that.

"Step carefully into the centre of the boat as if there are eggshells."

"One hand for you and one for the boat."

"Feet apart and flexed knees."

"Sit in the middle, lightly."

MARY ROSE

After a few months of bar work. I had my ear to the ground for some fun. While at supper with friends on Hayling Island, I had a chance encounter with the Mary Rose. A few friends had been invited to join us. They were all volunteer divers and archeologists working for the summer on the Mary Rose wreck in the Solent. Just a boat ride off Portsmouth Harbour. There seemed to be a problem with food.

"It's awful. All we get is cold plated meals in the kitchen."

"What?"

"Yep, they've employed this hotel caterer supplying meals. After two hours in the cold Solent we need something better."

"Someone is in trouble because the cold store was broken into and a fruit cake was stolen!"

I wondered, thought for a moment, then foolishly, I volunteered.

"I'll come and cook for you, it can't be that difficult."

"Really ... Can you cook?"

"[Scrambled eggs!] Yes. It *really* can't be that difficult ..."

"That would be great."

I heard later they gave me two weeks. I stayed all season through to the lift in October 1982. My days fell into a routine.

06.30 Butchers boat from Portsmouth Harbour dockside, next to The Ship pub, to Sleipner, moored over the wreck in The Solent.

Tiny cramped galley. Down steep ship steps with a handrail. Two gas burners and an oven, fridge. Larder and assorted cupboards. My home base. Hot. I thrived.

Prepare the day's food for 12 professional divers, 20 archeologists working round the tides ... lunch, biscuits, snacks. Order provisions for next day's delivery.

15.00 Butchers boat back to Portsmouth. If the tide and wind were right. Sail. I changed the food culture from forbidden to plenty. Plated meals and a locked larder. Out. Instead. Good healthy food available all day. Boxes of fruit, chocolate bars, biscuits, into an open larder. Help yourself. I cooked soups, pies, biscuits, and cakes. Left baked potatoes warm in the oven. We laughed.

"Do you want me to grate that cheese for our potatoes Susy?"

Divers worked the tides so needed food when they finished at different times. Onshore the purser had a market garden in Ramsey and as soon as he heard I was up for fresh produce, he sent daily deliveries. A box of fresh spinach produced mixed responses.

"I just love that spinach quiche!"

"I don't rate your green leaf pie!"

It was hard work but I was having fun. Forgetting myself. Trying to catch a husband. I can claim to be a cook by appointment too, informally. Prince Charles now King Charles was patron of the project and as an experienced diver, was a frequent visitor. The hoisting of the Royal Standard at appropriate moments caused much consternation for the crew. He came to dive with the team in very challenging conditions and usually stayed for lunch. Not mine.

"The royal party will be eating lunch provided by the sponsor on deck."

Cold vol au vent.

At lunchtime I heard a voice at the door of my very small galley.

"Can I eat what your divers are having?

"Yes sir, of course."

Baked potatoes, cheese, green leaf pie, salad by royal command.

What a summer in Portsmouth. 1982. Quivers of Tudor arrows found and tested for the first time. Lost varieties of apples, pips intact in the solent mud. Huge guns, knitted hose, barber surgeons caps only ever seen in oil paintings, delicate, fragile, entire. I was there. On board. Most days. It felt as if I was at the centre of things. Falklands War. Bloody Margaret Thatcher. Liners full of troops leaving and returning.

And then 'The Lift.' Late the night before. October. It was calm. Unusual. Equinoctial gales likely. Sleipner was dwarfed by a huge bright yellow crane poised ready to lift. To lift the Mary Rose clear of the water for the first time since the 1500's. Prince Charles was on board, and at midnight, dived with two chief divers. They were worried about the lift. A steel frame had been constructed around and under the ship. The word was that Prince Charles agreed to underwrite the lift. On Sleipner. Universal breath out. It could go ahead.

At two in the morning. The Mary Rose appeared on the surface for the first time. Early. Secretly. For us. A very low tide. Silently we watched. Margaret Rule, the project director, saw her.

"Tonight she is ours. Tomorrow she will be the worlds'."

6.00 am morning of the lift. I went on deck to see hundreds of small boats anchored around us, in a huge silent circle round wreck site. My skin tingled. The lift was live on TV.

As cook, I was learning about myself too. Positive mycelium. That enabling thread. Anticipation. Understanding what makes people flourish. More of these threads to come. First, tradition.

MARRIAGE

My search was over. My future husband was one of those professional divers, working on the Mary Rose. The day we announced our engagement a friend hurled a damp tea towel to the floor shouting:

"Brilliant, at last."

He was a bit like my dad. Public school, Ox-bridge engineer, large muscular, emotionally incompetent. Problem solver. Mostly silent. A gifted engineer. Valued me. Wore small tight speedo swimming trunks under his diving suit. He needed sex. I could do that. Not much warmth. November 1982. Our wedding. In Chichester register office and afterwards at a family friend's house, a widower from early West Pallant, Chichester family days. I think he was quite fond of my mum. There was pressure on her to marry again.

"I don't want to spend my life cooking supper and waiting in with warm slippers ready for an middle aged man to come back from the golf club"

Good stuff mum. I wish I'd paid more attention.

Mum was just brilliant. Still wobbly living alone. Now working as manager for a Citizen's Advice Bureau. She organised everything for my wedding. My father insisted he attend my marriage celebrations with his 'new wife and baby'. My mother said nothing. She held herself together. How dare he?

"What do you think you are doing? Have you no sensitivity to mum and me. How dare you think it's alright to bring your new baby to my wedding!"

I said nothing.

I have a picture from the wedding. Just one. For years I couldn't look at it. I didn't show it to Sarah. Didn't talk about it. I left it, forgot about it. In the loft in the stiff brown edged folder with gold edges. A wedding photograph. Signing the marriage register. My father is standing on the left. Smallest, Slightly crooked with his arthritic new hip. In a smart grey suit from Marks and Spencers. I can't remember his shirt or tie. He's looking down at the register.

"Susy off my hands ... great ... "

My new husband sitting next to me was also suited in grey. Leaning in smiling.

His father is standing on the left. Tall patrician, an eminent professor of medicine and mathematics. No visible emotion. Knighted for his work pioneering thyroid cancer treatments. Sir Edward. Widowed.

I'm in a cream skirt and silk striped blouse. No trainers. Poised hesitant. I'd done it. Married. I had ticked the box. Marriage. Everyone pleased.

We moved to Yorkshire. I'd done it. Married. I had to keep reminding myself. There seemed to be a general sign of relief. The next bit, done. Enfolded into society norms. Surname changed, my identity subsumed. I followed. Lived his life not mine. Lost myself. After the sex and honeymoon, I discovered he had black moods. The lack of care. But I could cope. MMO11. For days and days. I learnt to scuba dive to impress him. I could keep pace with his adventuring. In Yorkshire, the cottage was a builders yard. Unfinished. I drove to Guisborough market in an old Land Rover with a blanket and shovel in the back in case of snow. Waited for his return from North Sea diving work, three weeks on, three weeks off. Put mouse traps down in the kitchen. Walked. Cried. Laughed with gentle village neighbours. Sid was one. Retired now, a shepherd to his boots.

"I've noticed you do a lot of walking so I cut you a hazel thumb-stick. I whittled it smooth and cut it to your size. It should keep you steady over them 'ills."

"That's beautiful. Thank you."

I still have that stick. It felt just right in my hand. Smooth. Balanced. A lacrosse stick?

I wrote weekly letters to a friend with leukaemia. Ate lemon buns in Whitby. Dived on the remains of an Armada wreck in the Shetlands. We lived off farmed salmon and lamb. I passed myself off as the happily married woman. In role. Dressed to fit. Even had 1980's shoulder pads. I tried home making. We took a trip to Australia and New Zealand and he came back grumpy and complaining. I ran endlessly over the moors, dodging sheep with lambs on the steep lanes. Completed the York half marathon. I was lonely. I was trying hard to enjoy married life. I pretended. I walked alone around the moors, camping with the sheep. I didn't want to acknowledge the dark side of my husband at first. Days not speaking. Refusal to finish the cottage. His rages and throwing of tools when he was frustrated. He didn't harm me, but it was miserable at times. During his diving shifts on the oil rigs. I drove for 6 hours and 300 miles south to friends on Hayling Island. As often as I could.

BREATHING SPACE

I found breathing spaces ...

I went to visit my dad in Lancashire. He had a colleague for dinner. Sailing came up.

"I own a sailing boat that I keep at Lytham St Annes and I'd like to sail it up to Ballachulish."

"Where's that?"

"Scotland, just north of Oban."

"That sounds exciting. Dad, isn't Oban where you used to navigate your Corvette enroute to the north Atlantic convoys?"

"Yes they took all the navigation lights away, so it was tricky."

"I'm looking for crew for my trip ..."

"I'd love to come as a crew ..."

"Have you sailed before ...?"

"Yes ... some"

"... Susy is an experienced sailor, dinghies all her life and the Ocean Youth Club and there's ... Biscay, Portugal ... she is a great cook too."

"What type of boat is she ... ?"

"A Contessa 32 ... I am hoping two more friends will be able to join us, making a crew of four."

"Thanks, I'd love to come with you."

"I'd be delighted to have you."

"Depending on the weather we will leave next month, March, so we can get her up there for the summer."

Excellent. Escape. Sailing.

Lytham St Annes a few weeks later.

"Are we all set?"

"Susy you can have the forward bunk, Bob and James will have the cabin and I'll be in the navigator's berth."

"I've cooked a fruit cake for the trip."

"Thanks Susy, that's lovely. Bob, how will that be for you?"

"My heart condition might mean I'll have to go easy on it, although I just love fruit cake."

We nicknamed it angina cake.

"Harnesses on when sailing and clip on at all times on deck. Remember to stow everything in lockers."

"It will be an interesting passage. Our route is north of the Isle of Man then putting in enough westerly to get through the north passage between Ireland and the Mull of Galloway. Then west round the Mull of Kintyre leaving Rathlin Island well to port. We are exposed to the Atlantic there, so we may hit big seas before we get into the shelter of Islay and then Jura. We could make for Port Ellen depending on how we are doing."

Out of Lytham we headed north into the Irish Sea. A south westerly breeze.

"Ok we'll go with mainsail with a reef and the jib."

"We'll work watches two at a time."

Our routine was established. We enjoyed the Contessa 32. She handled beautifully.

"She's very responsive, lovely to sail."

"I could helm all day ... "

"You might have to!"

"In a big sea she's wet but will ride waves ok."

Tea and cake. More sailing.

"All hands on deck please!"

"Ok, we need to prepare for big seas to come. The next few hours out of the lee of Jura could be rough."

"I want all three of you in the cockpit clipped on and I'm going for'ard to take the jib down."

"Ok all ready."

A huge wave broke over the bows of the boat. Our skipper disappeared under it, and it swept aft soaking us all.

"Are you still there, skip?"

"Yep, phew, I was clinging on to the shroud and saw it coming ... just in time."

We reached Ballachulish intact. Firm friends. Trips to St Kilda and the longest spinnaker run of my life, so far, followed.

SKIN THREAD - SAILING DARTFORD

Late August 2018. Six months before the first signs of skin. My sibling connection continues to strengthen.

Hi dys,

Would you fancy sailing with us back to the Solent in Jedanor from Dartmouth?

The weather looks good for the next few days, so if you can get down soon it would be great.

We are moored at Dittisham, up the Dart River.

xxx ydes

Hi des,

Yes ... I'd love to. I'll see if I can get a train down to Totnes, I'm sure Catherine will help if she's there. I'll let you know.

xx ydys

What fun. Catherine was just brilliant. Ever encouraging. She knew how I loved sailing. Waiting for my delayed train at Totnes station at tea time she was there, smiling. Later that evening, in the pitch dark, we navigated narrow Devon lanes to find Jedanor moored in a small creek on the River Dart. Waiting. Ready to go.

"Get your warm clothes and oilskins on Susy, we are doing a night passage."

"We'll set off now to catch the ebb of the Dart."

Our passage along the coast was smooth and uneventful. Time for conversations with Jane.

"What sort of gravy do you like?"

"Oh it *has* to be thin. Gran used to do thick stuff and mum did that too. I can't stand it!"

"Thick is my favourite, with rice."

I had with me, a small soft favourite dog. Dill dog. Nearly Dindy. Jane sent me a framed picture of me with Dill dog.

"Susy and friend, 09.45 1st September 2018. Off Portland Bill."

Later, I am sitting having late Sunday breakfast in the cockpit of Jedanor anchored in Newtown Creek on Sunday 2nd September 2018. Fresh bread, cut roughly from a new baked loaf bought from a little place ashore, with just melted enough for spreading butter, thick to bite into, and chunky homemade marmalade with a hot mug of real coffee, freshly plunged.

On Saturday evening, we had arrived giddy, unwashed and slightly sleepless after our night/day passage. A heavy sea at The Needles. Finally navigating to our safe anchorage before the tide turned. Large glasses of malt whiskey, a damp boat ride ashore, a late meal of Italian pasta and wine eaten on a packed pub rooftop, we collapsed into our bunks, late, pissed, tired, and content. The following morning I was due to leave, job done. Then Jane asked me to stay ...

"We have been wondering if you would like to stay with us for another day and night and go back on Monday. You might enjoy helming some more too. We thought we could beat up to Newtown Creek this morning and anchor at the top of the tide. We could swim and have a lazy day before taking you to Cowes to catch the ferry on Monday. Would you like to, we'd love to have you?

To myself ... "gosh and wow, *really*?"

"Yes I would love it, thanks."

Into the Solent, a challenging beat, heeling in a good breeze, spray over the bow, me at the helm ...

"See if you can judge the tacks to get us into Newtown?"

"Ok, you are on."

We had the most glorious, wet, exhilarating sail. Tacking up the Solent, with wind and tide with us. I was faced with judging the time and place of the final tack, which would take us into

Newtown Creek, gentle light touch, concentration and feel, sensing the boat and the power of the sails. Columbus. My father had it, Jane too, now I showed I had it too. My heart sang with joy.

"Ready about, lee oh!" ... the final tack ... I made it. High fives and smiles. Sailing and my sister. Perfect.

I wrote a poem, later.

Invitation to stay
sparkling sunny morning
deep joy
warm sibling welcome
held with humour and care
deep joy
sailing challenge taken
precision, tacks and tide
deep joy
swimming, wine, talking
lives retold, reheard
deep joy
Bread, rice and gravy
1.50 and 3.05 games
deep joy
four years; too long
not any more
deep joy
for my des from your dys[1]

---

[1] Poetry: www.sueorton.co.uk

Back in Yorkshire in 1983 while training for a half-marathon one frosty morning. I found Botton Village, one of the first Camphill villages to offer supported living opportunities to adults with learning disabilities and special needs. They also had a thriving weaving centre. Floor looms and hand looms. I volunteered. Checks passed. I walked over the hill down into the Dale. Wrapped up against the cold. Hesitant at first ... gentle introductions. Possibilities ...

"What's your name?"

"Susy. I live over the hill in Westerdale."

"Can you help us with the weaving?"

"I can learn ... what do you need help with?"

Imbolc. My rekindling. Gentle helpful education and weaving. They would be my lifelines. Heart-lines. My weekly fix.

Courage was reignited too. Yorkshire was bleak. Marriage was bleak.

"I think we need to finish the cottage and move back South."

"No, I can't do that."

"The downstairs has been a building site ever since we moved back here. That's two years. I can't live like this."

"I'm going to get help to finish it."

"No you are not. I'm going offshore again for a month."

With help reluctantly received, we finished the cottage and sold it. Silent rage. Anger permeated everything.

"Why don't we move back South where we met. You have diving connections and family and so do I?"

We moved. Found a house in Havant. The house soon became another building site. I went back to university enrolling on an Advanced Diploma in Education: Special Educational

Needs. After my course, I worked at a Special School Leavers course in Portsmouth.

"We do a lot of Duke of Ed. But it's always a disappointment because they can't do the expedition bit and get their Bronze Award."

"Why can't they do it?"

"Confidence mainly, they can't navigate and it's too risky, students might get lost."

"Right."

I started. Working with six students. We walked out of the college together. They took a polaroid camera and a street map. No mobile phones then. A short route round the streets and back. Every few hundred metres we stopped.

"What can you see?"

"Post box. Street name. Bus stop. Tree. Traffic moving past."

"Take pictures of fixed things that will help you remember where you are."

"Phone box. Yes, good. Bus stop, great."

Clipping the pictures together in the order of the walk, we went out the following week. I said nothing. We found our way back to base. Smiles.

"Yippee, we did it." The next week they went out without me.

"Wow. Miss we did it, we didn't get lost."

It worked. We developed the length, the complexity of finding their way together. Added sound to the pictures. Descriptions of key places. Pairs. Small groups. Helping each other. Then a trip to the New Forest to work in the same way in the country. Anxiety. They put up tents together. Tangled ropes. Bruised fingers. More tents up together. Looked too baggy. Lost pegs. Again, tents up. In pairs. Better. Confidence. Laughter. Nerves. Anticipation. Expedition. Assessment.

"Do you think we can do this Miss?"

"Yes. I do. You will be fine."

"I am pleased to announce that all the students undertaking their expedition have passed the assessment."

The excitement at Portsmouth Guild Hall that July evening was the best.

"All my family are here, Miss."

"I have never *ever* been up on a stage to be presented with anything ever before. Never!"

"I am pleased to present to the students of Portsmouth Further Education College their Duke of Edinburgh Bronze Awards. Please come up onto the stage one at a time."

"It's amazing Miss ... will you be in our family picture?"

For years ex-students would stop me in the streets of Portsmouth. Proud. Smiling. Confidence up a notch or two.

Then I met her. I didn't mean to. I thought it had gone away. I thought the closet lid was tight. I hoped the lid was tight. It wasn't tight enough. Desire leaked through. But she was straight. I could still hide. Like wisps of blossom on a Spring breeze, the first scent of new mown grass. I tried so hard not to feel it. But it was there. I lied too. A managed denial. Unreasonable behaviour was enough, and he agreed.

Jane asked me last year.

"Susy, why did you go off with her ... "

"Because I fell in love."

"Oh ... "

My husband didn't guess.

"You just want to go off with the lawyer Greg don't you?"

Don't
So good the vow to stay away
from straight gorgeous women
too much for the weather in winter
stay cool, cold and don't, just
don't, don't even think about it!

I moved out.

A very painful, acrimonious divorce followed. I fought hard for a small settlement for my 10 years.

NOW WHAT

So far so conventional. A straight, straightforward life. Married. Lived in Yorkshire in a remote village. Cottage unfinished. Mice. Cold. Now Divorced.

Now I was off piste. Here's a recap. After straight laced boarding school, I followed the maternal family pattern into teaching and went to PE college. Third rate. South. No reputation for lesbians. Then taught in a London comprehensive. Far too constrained for me. Clause 28 looming. So I kept moving. Safer. Denial. There was sex, sailing, fun, laughter and lots of life and work. Fed Prince Charles and King Constantine of Greece while cooking for the raising of the Mary Rose.

"Would you like mustard on your ham sandwich, Sir?"

What mycelium lay in Yorkshire? Denial certainly. Courage and patience, yep probably. It took a while to get south, then out. What else? Botton Village for weaving and special needs teaching ...?

Sailing certainly held firm. Scotland trips. To St Kilda and that longest spinnaker run I've ever had to The Butt of Lewis. It makes me realise sailing and the sea is a strong creative family thread. Important. Connecting. Revealing. Palpable. Constant. A real, physical, geographical need and unconscious family escape to joy. All of our lives. My dad. My mum. My sister too. Tales of racing and escape. Of voyages and contemplation. Danger and jeopardy. Holidays and laughter. They are all there. Like homing birds we have all gravitated to water. To the edge. Away from the north, definitely the wrong place.

I now see that times when I was alone and frightened, I would find my way to a boat. Times when I was trapped and needed escape, sailing helped. Times when I needed reassurance and connection, helming boats was a language of reconciliation. Each and one of us. Sometimes. Together and often apart.

I was captivated, bewitched, but not out of the closet. I didn't tell my family. She wasn't a lesbian. She was 'church'. Sinful. Out of convention, into denial.

Much later Jane said:

"Mum and I were really worried about you."

I was probably worried about myself too, but far too busy falling in love, then slowly hacking my way out of the jungle. Luckily my positive creative inclinations and desires began to blossom too. Working as a consultant humanistic educator, I loved working in action. I took my talents to facilitating commercial organisational team building and change management in a forest centre in New Forest. I thrived and was asked to teach on an MBA at Southampton University. [not university material eh?] Received great feedback. I still didn't swallow it.

"Sue is just an inspirational facilitator."

I also rekindled and valued my love of making.

Where did I find this creative thread? Not at school. MMO11 missed that. After I left school, I had learned how to make my own clothes with my mum's old manual Singer sewing machine. I had watched my mum, happy in making. Sculpture. In her separation she had returned to painting. She would disappear for days. Sketch books. Concentration. Flow.

So one day, just like that, I realised I would love making baskets. Botton Hall remembered. I am practical. Sailing knots. Intriguing.

One favourite wedding present returned with venom was 'Ashley's Book of Knots'.

"You thought this would keep us tied together, well it hasn't!!"

So I enrolled on a basket making course in Dorset. I recorded the experience in a journal. 5th November 1997.

BASKETMAKING

It's settling, calm. Time has swept past. Weaving willow. Bending, french randing, waling, slyping, upsetting. Choosing butts and ends to match. Hands knowing. Aching anew. Smiling tired with the delight of it all. The feelings overwhelm me. My basket. My basket. It's really strong and secure, natural, unboiled skin on willow. Willow laying beside willow. I have waited so long to make this basket. My hands and eyes knew what to do. I can remember all the terms, the names and the types of weaving. Effortless. Flow. Didn't they make baskets in Lancashire? Weaving certainly. I have only ever remembered sports stuff easily before. As if I've done it before - coming home to my family of makers, using my hands. I am absorbed like never before. A simple strong passion in the making of my first basket.

Another thread strengthened. I found courses and basket making groups. Nurtured my slow developing creative self. Like sailing. In the gaps.

INCHING ALONG

Eventually, I plotted my escape

I will mix metaphors. I was a newly fledged lesbian, only to myself at the start. Slowly whispering louder as I found likely allies. I was developing my gaydar, although 'lesbiandar' would be more accurate. Allowing my intuition to sense, to tune in to seek out other lesbians. Those allies amongst you, lesbians particularly, may relate to this. I tried to explain in my writing group recently.

"Sue, you talk about being safe now, what does that mean?"

"I have always felt safe in this country."

If you can't see 'difference' how do you know? How do you find out if you can reveal yourself and be truly you? I want to write this in capital letters because it is the nub, the crux, the essence. Very tangled mycelium.

In 1989 I was only just out of the conventional marriage nest. Yes. Hard to remember, even to think about. My recent writing journal reflects this.

*This is the most difficult part of my life to untangle. Years with a woman who was not a lesbian. Hiding from my family. It's so, so painful. For years I have wondered two things: what made me stay so long in the relationship, and what was I getting out of it? There must have been something. I made a list. A house for free. Useful. Lots of care and attention. She was a wonderful cook, hospitable. Singing together. I enjoyed that. I guess I liked being wanted and cherished. Yet, I allowed myself to be controlled. Her family took priority, not mine. Just like in my marriage, my leap into a relationship had clouded her personality. She had agendas for me. Hers. Church. Spending my money. History of depression and denial. No lesbian, but loving the attention. Controlling, quick to jealousy and manipulation. Ahh!!!! Not an outdoor woman at all. She was beautiful. I tried. But I let go of many threads of me. **No sailing**!*

Once the dust had settled. I managed to nurture my instincts for holistic education and enrolled on a course that was to change my professional life. At the education department at Guilford University, in an old Nissen hut, attached, but not fully embraced by the education department, a course had been developed by the Human Potential Resource Group ... a course called Facilitator Styles ... it was all about the processes involved in learning. We learnt as a peer learning community ... an interview ... in ... we met in a big group circle every Friday. I felt right at home. Soon another's lesbiandar was activated.

"Are you a lesbian?"

Without any hesitation ... "Yes."

I think I was more surprised than they were.

I also began learning about being alive to my feelings, showing them, getting angry, laughing, crying, standing my ground and this thing called 'process' in groups. I also began having fun with poetry.

To process with or after
that is a question.
Is it better to do it after that
than to muddle it with that, perchance?
How much more do I remember
then and truly know, that at
the time to be confused?
If that is yours and then
that interjection is an interruption
is it time to point it out with
theory or with self - But yet
lo! how I honour your process
but this is by knowing if it's yours
or but the process. Forsooth
my own I know not but that
it be mine not yours.

Much later I wrote a book about process.
'.... all the things which happen in communication between individuals ... but not the actual words. Process occurs as a result of the words. We often feel it rather than see.'

We had a creative module. I thought I might make baskets. Impractical. Instead, I offered my poems, written on the train from Havant to Guildford. I read some out loud.

"These are very good Sue, I know the poetry editor for a publishing company. I think she might be interested in these, why don't you send them?"

I faltered. I sat. Not brave enough to believe my poetry was any good. So I didn't send them. My self esteem was growing, but it was not very strong, yet.

FAMILY

Meanwhile, Family. 1990's. My father had remarried. I went to his wedding, wishing not to. Afraid to say no. Then they swiftly moved to Devon and had a child, Emily. Marvellous. Bloody marvellous. My mother was trying to thrive, managing a Citizen's Advice Bureau. Busy. Travelling. Painting. Jane was busy, her family expanding, Polly, Sarah and then Tom. She was working hard too, making radio shows. Founding a housing association. Her husband retraining as an architect.

Later, one night in November my father rang to arrange his visit before Christmas. He came alone, usually, and I enjoyed that.

"This year I'd like to bring Emily with me."

Feeling brave enough to stand my ground ...

"I'd really rather you didn't, I enjoy seeing you by yourself once a year."

"That's so selfish. You are being very unreasonable."

He was very angry.

"I'd like you to come alone, dad."

He slammed down the phone.

That night he had a massive stroke. Six months later he was dead. His funeral in Devon was a deeply sad, unsettling, upsetting affair. Jane and I drove down together. With my niece Sarah. Quietly remembering ...

"I don't have much to remember dad ... I've moved too much ... "

"Would you like my signet ring, he gave it to me but I'd like you to have it."

A beautiful gesture. I took it off during my skin time, but it's back on now. I love it and Jane for her kindness.

My mother was not mentioned at the funeral.

At the graveside, in the cemetery at Instow church, with a view of his beloved sea, I was pausing, gently saying my goodbyes alone, quietly, sobbing. A strange man, Ethne's brother I think said ...

"I think you have had enough time there ..."

"Fuck off ..."

LESBIAN

Being a *lesbian* unacknowledged, unspoken, a dread of my inner thoughts. For much of my life. I had thought it would go away. But it didn't. Over the years the denial and survival carapace I had developed was thick, strong and resilient, it was also to become my blind spot. My survival was to keep moving and not to value myself. To move on, not to stay anywhere. I was awash with shame for so long I didn't even realise it. I kept moving.

"You have the most number of addresses of anyone in my address book Susy." Jane in 1998.

Woven into these years there are the positive threads of me. I began my crawl out of the closet into the light. Slowly. Painfully. I was getting braver. Gaydar working. I began to meet other lesbians not dressed in tweed. I found opportunities. A workshop. Discrimination Matters. We did an exercise called 'stand up and sit down' to identify our differences and similarities. Stand up if you identify with any of these groups ...

"Left handed ... right handed ... lives in Southampton ... that's most people here ... drives a car ... ok not so many ... identifies as vegetarian ... ok ... living alone ... has children ... is a sister ... a mother ... married ..."

"Anyone who identifies as lesbian or gay?"

I didn't stand up, but I knew I wanted to. It was closer.

I looked at the people who did stand up. I paused. Something stirred within me. They looked normal enough ...

My professional life was improving too. My F- styles expertise facilitating process was recognised by the director of an outdoor centre in Beaulieu. I specialised in working with commercial clients. Work flourished. I met Sarah there. She was different. A playmate. We worked together. Laughed together. We organised and ran Wild Women in the Woods courses in the

New Forest together. Women together. Groups of women together, gay and straight. I liked this.

"Don't worry about going up into the high ropes course, we can get you down from anywhere!"

She would come and stay with me and bring wine and copies of Diva, unsure of my sexuality.

"When I came to stay, I was not sure you were a lesbian."

I wasn't sure then either. Not quite brave enough. Yet. I was only just learning lesbian signals.

We continued to work together. Lots. Friends commented that we seemed to sparkle together. Then, she moved to Reading and I moved to Swindon. We lost touch.

SAIL WITH JANE

Luckily for me, Jane unconsciously sensed something was amiss ... remember, she and mum were worried, and she beat up Pamela Wrigglesworth. She asked me to go sailing. A small significant catalyst for my final step from my closet. Little did she know ... I was living in Winchester. Out of the blue, a call ...

"Do you fancy a sail from Chidham today Susy?"

"Really ... Oh yeah ... I'd love it."

"You can't possibly go sailing, I'm cooking Sunday lunch!"

"I'm going."

"When will you be back?"

"I don't know. Sailing is unpredictable. Tides. Breeze."

"The lunch will spoil."

"Probably ... "

"Meet you there at 10 Jane."

Two up in a Laser, force 3-4 together, we took off into the Bosham Channel. Exhilarating. Frightening. But it was so, so important. Family. Jane shouted.

"It might be a bit more windy out of the lee of Cobnor in the southwesterly ... "

"Ok!"

"We'll get wet too ... "

"Yes!"

I ate my Sunday lunch, cold at 6.0pm. In silence. Perfect.

Courage was building. Confidence too. I needed to step away from this relationship. But there was fierce resistance. A repetition of my divorce. Painful. Tearing away, again.

"I'm leaving you."

"No you're not. You're ill. Depressed."

"I'm not, I'm leaving."

Possessions thrown onto the street. Tears. A return. Eventually, I left. Homeless, I called a dear lesbian friend ...

"I need a safe place to stay, do you know anyone with a room?"

Felicity and Rob have a room. Brilliant. I could breathe out.

Today there were two jobs
today there is a new dimension
    today there is a glimpse
        round the corner
today I am unsure
today I am in a new place
a valued and challenged place
today I am unsure and a little
frightened by the possibilities
today I must negotiate
today I must sit with
being unsure
today I must sit still,
and not panic.

SARAH

I continued my work at Beaulieu, further developing the MBA module for Southampton University. I was enjoying myself. Revelling in working with difficult commercial clients and their teams.

One spring day my life changed.

"Can you make the Safety Day in March at Beaulieu this year Sue?"

"Yes I'll be there."

"How would it be if you took a commercial team that day around the Safety Day ... they could be a bit of a challenge and I trust you?"

"OK, that's fine. Who else will be coming?"

"All the usual crowd. I think you know Sarah don't you? She's back in touch, so she'll be there."

We gathered in the Wood. All milling about. Catching up. Anticipating the day. I was deep in conversation with a colleague when Sarah came up.

"Hi."

We just stood together. Time slowing down. Looking. Smiling. Connecting. Together. Smiling. Coffee breaks. Together All through the social evening. Close. Newly inseparable.

"Why don't you come and stay with me in my flat?"

"I'd love to."

"Let's make it a weekend in a week or so ... ?"

A few days later ...

"I need to postpone our weekend as I'm off windsurfing to Margarita for two weeks ... "

"... that sounds fun, see you when you get back."

Reconnected. Sparkle ignited. Wow. With no agenda for me, just fun and laughter. She lived alone in Sussex in a small flat by the sea. Windsurfing. Her passion. Her joy. I wanted to live alone, independently, to find my feet, so I bought a flat in Portsmouth. And a second hand Solo dinghy. The road between us became very familiar at weekends.

Then we went to the fireworks together in 1999. Several years later, we bought a house together by the sea. Home. Sarah became the love of my life, my partner and my safe ground on which I could find my lesbian feet, my self worth, my creative heart, and flourish. I let go of a lifetime of being frightened of fireworks.

*If I told you
that I felt safe to fall
then I would say it.*

*If it were simply to be
grateful for much rest and
recuperation
then I would say it.*

*If cuddling cats, warm sheets
and square pillows were just right
then I would say it.*

*If tender care, food for my soul
described it
then I would say it.*

*If however, I wanted to tell you that
you held me around
a corner of my life,
I would not know how to say it.*

I secured a full-time job in 1998 as a National Learning and Teaching Adviser first at Southampton University then at Sussex University in 2000. I realise now that I was trying to prove something, prove I was intelligent, prove I could mix it with academics, prove to my family, to myself and prove to Miss Turner, at MGC 1969, that she was wrong.

"I am afraid, Sue *is* university material."

I was thrilled. Good salary. Proper job. I flourished for a while. Yet, I was still aware of a reluctance, a hesitation to value myself. I avoided talking at big events and tried to keep under the radar. My colleagues were supportive and encouraging and I flexed my facilitation muscles wherever I could. I met Neill, Head of the Teaching and Learning Centre. He really valued my work. I felt warm about that. Thawing out ever so slowly.

Professors could be challenging.

"Now, we are going to get into pairs to discuss the learning strategies which will enhance and improve student learning."

"I don't need to talk about that. My lectures that I have presented for years are *quite* sufficient. I have never had any complaints."

" That's fine you sit out ... everyone else is going into pairs to discuss learning strategies ..."

"Ridiculous, what a waste of time, I know what I am doing."

"... We *are* going into pairs to discuss learning strategies... "

Everyone happily went into pairs to discuss learning strategies ... He joined a pair a little later ...

"That was quite useful ... actually."

I'm sitting at a lecture
obedient at the back
no-one seems to realise
the boredom.

I co-wrote a book too. All about groupwork skills explaining process. I am proud of it. Now in its third edition. I also gathered kindred spirits there. Neill among them. Many still, firm friends.

All of us are determined to support student centred learning. Collaborative, enjoyable, puzzling, body, soul, emotion, heart, brain everything jumbled up together learning.

Hierarchy didn't really get it. It was hard. Pushing rocks uphill. I was beginning to hate it. Only my head was valued. The bit above my eyebrows. The rest of me didn't matter, wasn't even seen.

I realised that my mountain climb to prove myself was not even worth the view. It was exhausting, debilitating. Corridors full of closed, name plated doors and men [mostly men] behind them. Exams and experts persisted.

When I was eventually bullied for my process knowledge by an engineering professor, I fell over. I was given three months off

    to recover by a supportive GP.

WEAVING - MUM

Journal entry:
I feel as if I have been dumped in a dark forest with a sack over my head.

Morning tea became a special place for me, a healing place. Struggling without sleep or inner safety, anxiety would drive me to get up, wrap up, get warm and make tea. Early. I'd also make a small snuggly hot water bottle, not too much water, but squeezed flattish so it was thin enough to tuck into the small of my back. Baggies on, my favourite blue woolly hat, soft socks, I would hold my mug close. Then, finding a cosy sofa to sit on, snuggle in, awake, watchful, I'd try to settle, to calm, to breathe, to wait, to try and wait until I could drink my tea. It was hard. Sarah called it grains of sand time. Nothing happened, but it was the beginning of something. Some might call it healing or mindfulness, but then for me it was only waiting for my tea to cool. I did nothing, yet something within me changed. Cells relaxing or blood flowing slower, my breathing unconsciously gentle and easing, anxiety falling away, perhaps. At the beginning I would run out of patience and put cold water in my tea, get up, stay anxious. Then each day I added minutes to my sitting trying to wait, trying not to try but waiting just the same. I don't remember how long it took me to wait for my tea but I did. One day I waited long enough to drink it. Mycelium.

I thought about my mum. Her creative life. I wondered about her creative life, because I seem to have lost mine. My mum was ill with a long endured lung disease which was slowly killing her. Yet in retirement, she painted; she loved it. She could disappear for days into painting absorbed in the colour, the form, the detail.

"Don't bother trying to ring me for the next couple of days, Susy, I have a series of sketches which I want to put onto canvas. I'm trying a new technique with just three colours."

This deep need to make, emerged from this depression and denial. I remembered wisps of desire for a more creative life all through my life, but I never could or had the courage or resources to follow them. I realise now that creative education somehow didn't see me, so for a long time I didn't see myself. Education had unconsciously separated my head from my heart and soul. During those married years, in the gaps, I had sought patches of sunlight to warm my heart. I had pushed my making instincts and skills into the side, into weekend courses, to 'hobby' status. I could make beautiful baskets, woven with willow and rush ... now I wished for colour, cloth weaving ...

I went to see mum.

"Of course I understand completely. I am an artist too."

She encouraged me to buy my first second hand table loom... I learnt by instinct, by taking it apart and rebuilding it ... I began to hear and feel my own creative heart beat.

A part-time Psychodrama Diploma brought me back to life, healed my facilitation muscles and helped me to be seen, to confront and dive through some trauma and shame. Releasing. Brilliant. At a conference there I met Noelle. Irish but living near me. Joy. Now a dear friend, kindred spirit and creative work partner. I think we have probably known each other since childhood or in another life ... it felt like that. She was to become a vital ally through my skin shedding. With colleagues from Sussex I worked as a learning and teaching consultant, mentoring modern musicians. It balanced with my weaving perfectly.

Then in 2012 my mum died. It wasn't sudden. COPD was relentless. Knowing she was going to die, she had prepared. Cleared the house. We talked. We hugged. I loved her. The last time. Out of hospital. Knowing she only had a few weeks. Into a care home, she had chosen for their experience with the final stages of her disease. Help with her dying. Her paintings on all the walls. Jane had negotiated with the doctor for morphine, to ease her pain, and more. She sat and waited, intelligent, aware ... I visited her ...

She was slumped in an unfamiliar arm chair, refusing her bed ... dozing ... blue eyes flashing as she heard me ...

"Susy ..."

My eyes filled ... "Mum ..."

"Your mum should be with us for a while yet ... "

Hands clasped, we sat together ...

"I love you very much, mum"

"I love you too Susy. But I don't know about this next bit ... "

"No ... "

"I'll see you in the morning."

She died at 9.00pm that night. I wasn't there.

The funeral was difficult. Jane didn't come. She wanted no funeral, just cremation. I insisted, and organised the funeral. I was sad she didn't come. I tried to keep the door open. Some of her family came. They read. I read. It was difficult without Jane. She was very angry with me. After six months, I wrote, reaching out for reconciliation. Jane reached back. A year later, after a simple heartfelt lunch together, we walked on the South Downs, scattering my mum's ashes on the slopes above Chichester.

Later, Jane would tell me she was proud of me for standing my ground about the funeral. It felt important, possibly the first time I had stood up to her.

DAMSELFLY

My first weaving commission. A request from the partner of my South Downs Tweed admirer.

"Do you take weaving commissions?"

I thought a while and then replied:

"Now, a commission ... the process of weaving for me, is to find some inspiration photographs, pictures, writing or something that intrigues me ... then to sketch, to explore shapes and ideas without knowing the form, colour or structure of a piece, until it 'emerges' out of my sketch books and pondering. Once this happens I play with colour and weave structure, sample some ideas on my small loom to develop a piece. Then when I'm happy I design a warp, wind it and then put it onto my loom before weaving and then finishing it. It seems to take about a month for each section. The summer is wonderful as I'm not mentoring too. In the autumn weaving is punctuated with a couple of weeks mentoring each term. So if we were to discuss a weaving for E, I would suggest the same process... and I wonder ... she has sent me her Damselfly poem and I am pondering and digesting that in my coffee breaks by our pond [hoping to see a damselfly!] could that perhaps serve as inspiration for a scarf? or something else she loves ..."

We collaborated beautifully. Exchanged ideas. Woven. Finished. Folded into pale blue tissue paper, boxed, packed. In time for Christmas. I hear nothing on 25th and by January gremlins of doubt. I text ...

"Did you get Damselfly?"

"Oh Sue ... did you not get my rapturous text on Christmas day? I'll take a screenshot of it to send you."

"I absolutely love it. I feel incredibly privileged to have such a beautiful piece of art created for and with me, and one that I can wear as well. Our house (1930s single brick) is bitterly cold in the winter, despite radiators, so my Demoiselle gets much use in

the evenings. But she lives primarily in my study where I write much of my poetry - a kind of muse garment. I'm still discovering her in all her aspects. And it is an especial delight to remember the choices I made, the images shared, the discussions had, to then see the artistic choices you have made : the slub, the soft pink, the more lime green, the hint of moss amongst the kingfisher / demoiselle iridescent blue. She is an ever-surprising persistent joy to my eyes." E x[2]

Weaving for me is as fine art, colour and pattern. Time spent looking. Wondering. Puzzling. Commissions come, slowly. It's in my hands and deep in my heart now. It's taken a long time to understand, value and practise the art of not knowing; my hands know. My hands. Yes. A lightness of touch. Feel. Natural to me. Lacrosse. Sailing. Willow.

"Your left hand does most of the work, hold the base of the stick lightly but firmly…your right hand guides, supports." Lacrosse.

"Ease the rod around the base sticks with your hands, feel where the line is." Willow.

"Don't grip the boat's tiller, gently now. It's all about the feel." Columbus.

Flow. When time just disappears. Artists often begin something without knowing how it will turn out. In practice this translates as thinking through doing. Some methods can seem counterintuitive or irrational: distraction or relinquishing control, embracing chance and collaboration; following a hunch rather than a rationale; privileging the senses over the intellect… I'm a maker, baskets first and then in search of colour, weaving. I made Catherine a washing basket in 1996.

"I still use your basket every day."

Seeing it now when I visit makes me smile.

---

[2] Elvire Roberts: Poet: Instagram @laconicpicnic

POSITIVE THREADS

Positive threads. Sarah. Life. Sailing. Weaving. Writing. Swimming. Singing. Family. Consultancy work... all so good. Yet ... as friends gathered reminiscing about Lesbian Feminist days in the 1980's I hated it ... I froze, grumpy, silent again, gulps of denial ...

"What were you doing in the 80's Sue?"

... hiding but wishing I had not ... beating myself up for not being brave enough...

"Teaching... "

Into my head swims a myriad of stars
doubting, yes, dubious patriarchal certainty.
Where have women been?
Is there a primal scream for womankind?
The smell of burning flesh of many witches.
My sisters, burnt for speaking out.

ANNIE ALBERS

January 2019 I visited the Annie Albers exhibition at the Barbican. Annie was a weaver who had worked in the Bauhaus School. Her work was beautiful, simple, intoxicating.

"How does she do that? The threads are so fine. She only uses black red and cream but the effect is astonishing."

It took me by surprise, as I left the exhibition, smoothing down the crowded escalator, I realised I was crying, crying soft tears, full of relief, happy silent tears, I stopped. Realisation dawned. Why wasn't I weaving more? If I stopped working I could, I really could. I was tired of venture capitalists squeezing the life and soul out of my consultancy work at a music college.

"We are no longer paying staff for their travel time, we will pay your travel, but not your time."

Berlin? Dublin? Manchester? ... no thank you.

"Tutorial time is being reduced, and your hourly rate is going down."

I resigned. Stopped. Paused. Sat in my studio. Waiting for the relaxation of space and time for weaving.

It didn't come. My endurance was holding, but there were cracks. My inner voices ...

"Come on, don't be silly, buck yourself up ... you have time to weave and play at last."

"It's May Susy, go and sit on the beach, go for a swim, you can relax now ... "

I sat. Blue brilliant sea. Warm Spring sunshine. Space. Time.

Then tears, steady relentless tears. For two days ...

I thought of Catherine, now a retired psychotherapist, safe, lifelong, I called her. Upset. Puzzled.

"I've the space now, time. I can relax ... but I don't seem to be able to stop crying ..."

"I am not really surprised at your distress, you've had so much to deal with. In boarding school and in your early adult life especially. I have always thought of you as floating, like a leaf, not grounded, wandering, blown about and now I wonder if it might be helpful for you to explore finding your roots."

"Oh ... "

"I think Core Process therapy might suit you."

"Really ... How long?"

"Maybe a year or so."

I sat down ... a leaf ... no roots ...

Therapy was not new. I had spent many hours untangling and unpacking various life events, usually work related. But there was other stuff ... that closet, those decisions, that denial, that shame. I knew there was stuff. But too deep, too difficult and probably very painful.

Over the years I had developed a carapace, thick, strong and resilient; it would take a while to remove. I had remained silent throughout. I knew I was brittle and defended. Sarah knew.

"If I ask you a question, you sometimes snap my head off ... "

"*I don't!*"

I began the painful catharsis, the release of long buried unconscious lifelong trauma. Into my chrysalis. Slowly my long silent throat reached out to my heart. All my life I have trusted my body. My mum told me I could run before I was one; I am a physical being, trained in physical education. I run fast. My body just knows. Boarding school taught me to watch, to sense not to speak; I played sports, I ran and I felt things. I learnt then to trust and listen to my body. Did I trust my body? I had no idea what was to come.

So I chose a therapist trained in Core Process psychotherapy with craniosacral experience too. My craniosacral therapy continued in parallel.

I now know, that it was only because I had space, security and happiness that I could fall apart. Slowly I realised the volume and intensity of my tumblings through childhood, boarding school, family break up, closet life, marriage and lesbian denial. It had rendered me tough, defended and not very caring of myself. A blade buried. Wary and sharp. Imposter to myself. Unknowing and unwilling to rest in myself with ease. Unconsciously successful and talented. Seeping wariness. Until my 66th year. This was how I was. It was the me I knew inside. Not the me, I showed the world. But underneath. It was shocking yet a relief, a breathing out of me. I didn't know there was a softer, kinder, gentler me underneath. My skin had received this message too. I was holding something in.

My journal records.
June 4th therapy: Identified deep pain of boarding school (at 11) and the separation of my parents soon after; in all 20 years of trauma. I had remained silent throughout. I began the painful catharsis of this trauma release, and worked to open my throat chakra to my heart.

July 3rd in Suffolk 2019, on holiday. Three friends together to walk, to swim and explore. The cottage we rented pre-pandemic was small but compact. Cool inside for the summer weather, dark expensive but not very comfortable leather sofas. A slatted wooden table and chairs placed on the paved terrace at the back invited outdoor breakfasts and evening drinks. It was near a footpath tucked into woodland down a lane not too many miles from the sea.

"Can you look at my back, I've some itching in the small of my back where I can't reach?"

"There are two small patches, like a rash. They are small. It's probably nothing."

Two days later.

"I'm feeling a bit rough, my body aches. I wonder if it's related to that rash? I think I'll stay and watch Wimbledon tennis this afternoon. You two go walking."

First visible signs of my rash? Possibly. Hindsight is a precious thing. Then, I was ignorant of the journey I was facing. Now looking back there were many signs and signals, clues and events. But there it is, the puzzle. We walk backwards into our future.

"Those patches are still there, and now I have a rash on my chest and neck a bit too."

"Perhaps you should go to the GP."

"Ok. I'll do some research."

Hands feet, body eyes ... Intuition

July 2019 GP, two minutes looking at my raw inflamed body ... dismissive.

"It's definitely not Pityriasis Rosea. You need steroids to clear this. It's only a skin infection probably eczema. I'll give you steroid tablets [2 per day for 5 days] and antihistamine tablets."

"That should clear it."

Two days later, anxious, awake, at three in the morning, wondering ...

Journal: I've had a rash now for a couple of weeks now and it's getting steadily worse + me feeling rough too. Friday I went to the GP who in two minutes gave me cream (steroids) but wrong instructions and no emollient to put on before steroids... so put it straight onto my skin!! ... it's getting worse... Last night my skin was on fire so I showered the stuff off.

I'm not too good at trusting doctors. I hardly ever see them. Sarah's father was a doctor though, and she trusted western medicine more than me. I trusted her. Once when I went to a doctor in London with a very painful ear infection he asked me to take my trousers off... ?

"I need to get the penicillin into a big muscle in your thigh so it will work fast."

"Oh."

This time, three days of steroid creams...

"This isn't right, your skin is on fire. I think you should go back to the GP."

"I've booked with the practice nurse, will you come with me?"

Blood tests, all clear.

"Could it be Pityriasis Rosea?"

"It looks a bit like it. PR is usually a rash adolescents and young adults get and it's often anxiety related. It can last about 12 -14 weeks. We will give you more steroids with cream this time."

July 2019 Therapist
"Shedding trauma through your skin is a natural healthy process."

Over the summer I endured. After several weeks I stopped steroids. Decided a more gentle route was preferable. Natural cocoa butter. Swimming. Therapy. I hoped. I kept going. That was the old me. I could do that. We had holidays planned. Wales and Greece and then a women's gathering in Pembrokeshire.

"Will you be alright travelling to Wales?"

"Yes I'll manage."

I couldn't walk far. Slept with gloves and cream. Improvised washing up bowls to soak my painful feet. Cream. Gloves. Soak feet. Not very good company.

Eventually, back, chest, face, cleared. But my hands, feet and legs felt as if they were worse. I found that craniosacral therapy, Homoeopathy and therapy all helped.

Holiday in Samos. Our favourite place. Hot. Sea and pool swimming. I thought it might revive me.

"Do you think you could manage our favourite walk to Vourliotes ... we could start early so it's cooler?"

"Yes I'll manage. I'd like to try ... "

Determined. Slow. Distressed. Difficult.

"Press on!"

"I'm not sure I can make it back from here ... I need to sit in the shade ..."

Rest. Quiet. Pool swim. Long cool drinks. Exhausted. What the fuck is happening!

Home. I continued my summer routine of sea swimming, homoeopathy and cocoa butter, water, and plenty of fresh fruit and vegetables with no steroids. Most of my body was clearing. But not my lower legs, hands and feet. Despite all of this care and energy for healing, I became distressed. Something was holding on.

By late Autumn 2019. My diary records:
"melt down last night ... morning, hands cracking, dry, yellow, sore and itching, I can't hold a pencil ... feet - dry cracking with little toes bleeding and hurting ... shoes hurt so socks again ... what the fuck do I do with this ... it has been going on TOO LONG!"

Craniosacral wisdom suggested that the extremities were often the last to clear because they were not vital organs. Not vital unless you were a weaver, a writer, a walker, a runner. I was struggling. Minute by minute, hour by hour. By nature I am a positive creature. Bright side and all that. But this, this was wearing me very thin. What on earth did I have to do to clear it? My therapy continued to be deep and powerful, unearthing pain and distress from childhood, from boarding school and beyond. Closet shame, pain, distress in bucket loads dumped on the floor of that garden therapy room. There, I was beginning to see how well I had done in the face of such turmoil and oppression. Slowly slowly believing.

Standing at the Hove bus stop in the rain after a particularly hard, skin interrupted therapy.

"God, it was difficult. Cream on and gloves on to stop me scratching."

I had spent the summer confident that this skin condition was linked to trauma release. I was only now realising the extent of my long buried distress. Surely it was better out than in? Surely my skin was doing something healthy and positive? I breathed out. Could I keep going?

November diary
Extremely distressed and low - worse in the evenings. Damp wrists inside elbows and knees. Patches of red scaly skin on legs particularly knees and upper arms. Hands: permanently dry, cracking, irritated and sore. Cream temporary relief, gloves help a bit. Palms yellow and red swollen fingers. Feet: dried out, hard, very itchy -more than ever - heels and soles sore. Nails hard and ridged on hands and feet. It feels like I'm being tortured.

A family walk then 'Christmas lunch' in a popular crowded South Downs pub; Tables booked for twenty. Organised by Jane, all her family were there. First a walk.

I found each step painful. I was exhausted. My hands hurt, I had to wear gloves. My feet were painful. Bleeding socks. I was miserable but putting on a brave face. Where had I done that before? Jane noticed my distress.

"Susy, I can see you really struggling with your hands and feet. This skin thing has been going on too long. You need to go to a private skin specialist. I have the number of one to call."

BACK INTO NHS

The recommended specialist was busy until February. And very expensive. So I stepped back into the NHS. Reluctant. Via my new woman GP. I was referred to the local skin clinic.

I had an appointment with a skin specialist on 17th December. He was dapper, expensive shoes, a waistcoat and jacket. He was late. No apology. He didn't say my name or introduce himself after my 30 minute wait.

"Take your shoes and socks off."

"My rash is on my legs and hands as well. I've had it for ..."

"... just take your shoes and socks off."

He didn't meet my eyes, didn't see me. He didn't ask *anything*."

A cursory inspection of my feet.

"You've got Athlete's Foot."

"Are you sure! I've had this rash for ..."

"Of course I am sure, it's a classic case. I teach medical students you know and this is a classic case. Do you mind if I take pictures so I can use it in my teaching."

Statement not question.

"It's a classic case, easily treated."

"... but are you sure? I have a rash on my legs, damp skin ..."

His stare silenced me ... Who do these patients think they are? I'm the expert.

I knew. I'd met plenty of those in university. Ahhhh!

"We can have this cleared up in a week or so. I'll give you tablets and a cream."

"I'll just take a sample for the lab. We should have your results in no time. A classic case, students frequently misdiagnose this. We can have this cleared in no time.

Next!"

NOELLE

I was a year into recovery from Sussex University narrow-mindedness. Playful, at a psychodrama conference in Cirencester. Stepping into a sociodrama as an awkward adolescent, asked to leave their phone at the door. Bolshy. Fun. Later, high on the energy of dancing at the cèilidh. I stepped out into the balmy July evening where folk sat drinking. Seeing me they remembered my earlier performance ...

"Well now, have you left your phone at the door?"

"... no mate, I sneaked in an' took it back!!"

Laughter ...

"Do you want a drink ... ?"

Warm friendly welcome and banter. I sat with them.

"I am looking for psychodrama pals near where I live... "

"Where do you live?"

"Worthing."

"Bett! ... my sister ... she's lives in Worthing."

"Oh ... ok?"

"She was going to come to this but couldn't ... "

"I could be your pal ...

"... But you sound Irish? "

"Yes ... to be sure ... but I live in England ... near Southampton."

"Brilliant!"

"Let's meet ... somewhere in the middle, between us... Emsworth would be good. I've no idea where that is but I'll find it."

An all day lunch followed. So much common ground ... psychodrama, sociodrama ... process understanding, working in action, sport, playing and watching ... a kindred spirit ...

playful... in the moment. So English and so Irish... I could breathe out.

Sarah was sometimes puzzled by my work.

"I'm never quite sure how to explain what you do ... process facilitation ... it's hard to explain ..."

Noelle knew. She did process stuff too. Sociodrama training together followed. Trips to Manchester. To Oxford. Regular meetings in Havant. Meeting my mum. My confidence and expertise growing and expanding. Our consultancy Facilitation Matters - sprang from these beginnings. In action with us people often say "I hadn't thought of it like that before." We are still working together. Marvellous. Bloody marvellous.

One meeting in Chichester. On an outdoor field and adventure playground. Swings and stepping blocks. Pre skin. We were both a bit unsettled. Unsure. Action exploration needed. It is our core work ... don't talk about it, *show* me ... she stepped onto the playground ... walking, puzzling ... together we wondered in action.

"I miss my feet on the soil of Ireland ... oh dear... it's a deep ache ... how about a map ... walk on a bit of Ireland ... stand on it ... tears ... plans for a visit soon ... at home you could tune into Irish Radio ... be near coast, a plan ... yea that sounds good, I'll do that."

Then me:

"I'm feeling that my body is brewing something ... I'll just dance on these blocks ... foot to foot, foot to foot ... tears ... sobbing ... something is coming and I don't know what it is!"

We spend a lot of time 'not knowing' for each other and with our clients. Holding distress. Puzzling gently.

When my skin took hold. This friendship held too.

SKIN

After my specialist appointment I texted Noelle:

SO: Specialist made quick diagnosis, infection like athletes foot ... cream n tablets should clear it in 2 weeks 😠

NB Dear God... I'm not sure what I feel just reading that?!? 🤔 *Really so glad that you've come out with something clear & treatable & also somehow shocked by it?* 😲

I didn't get results. He went on holiday.

SO: I'm sad to report that my skin is far from healed ... it's been a tough Christmas with the treatment making me sick with a headache. I shall be going to the GP next week.

NB: Ah feck that Sue, so sorry that it hasn't healed for you yet 😔

On 31st December I reluctantly went back to my GP.

"I'm sorry to hear your skin has not cleared. There's an ex GP skin specialist running a clinic in Lancing who might help you. He may have appointments this week."

I checked. I knew him. Booked an appointment that day. I was fragile, but determined. Sarah came with me.

"How long have you had this skin rash?"

Dear God ... someone was asking me *again* ... so I repeated my story, bullet points, staccato, with feeling ...

- Skin rash patches on my back - late June
Then on face, neck, back ... to GP.

- GP 1 - steroid prescription no mention of emollient just a rash, easily cleared.

- Two days. Steroids ointment directly on my skin. Body, eyes, face on fire I was screaming ... I couldn't open my eyes.

- Practice Nurse ...

"We don't prescribe emollients, you have to buy that yourself ... Pityriasis Rosea "possibly?"
- GP 2 in for 2 minutes ...

Overheard conversation with nurse:

"This isn't serious ... it's just a rash it will clear. Give her steroid tablets."
- Steroid tablets for a fortnight. Not much change.
- My July lightbulb moment. "It's trauma releasing."
- Therapy and craniosacral professionals confirmation and understanding. A healthy process.
- July pictures. "Oh, that looks really painful"
- Stop taking steroids late July to allow trauma release.

Natural skin cream, cocoa butter and homoeopathy. Sea swimming
- Face, neck, back and chest are now much calmer. Yet, it was hanging on and on. And on!
- Trauma leaving vital organs. Extremities hanging on.
- Hands and feet sore itchy bleeding, lower legs red and itchy, sweaty and damp legs but no temperature.
- "Go to a skin specialist Susy"
- NHS Skin Clinic cursory glance by Dr - Athlete's Foot!
- Treatment over Christmas. Sickness, depression... anger.
- No lab results yet ... wit's end, tethers, had it ... all the cliches.
- GP 3 suggested you.
- Now I am here!"

I breathe out ...

He looks closely at my feet and hands.

"Mmmmm interesting ... this isn't Athlete's Foot! You might *have* athlete's foot but it's not the cause. It's a red herring!"

Really?

Sarah raises her eyebrows. Say's nothing. I breathe in ...

"I'm not sure what this is. It must be distressing. It could well be Pityriasis Rosea. I'm not sure."

... I hold my breath ... wait ...

"I think you need to try steroids twice a day to clear this. You will need to put an emollient cream on first."

Fuck ... Really! ... had he been listening?

"I've been round that loop in June and it wasn't very helpful."

"This really is the best treatment I can offer and with the emollient first it should be better. I'll prescribe both and give you cream, not ointment as it isn't so sticky."

Eyebrows up. Mutual nod. Sigh. Acquiescence. Tethers shortening.

"If it's the only thing?"

"Trust me."

"You will get the prescription from your GP in a day or two."

Steroids. again. Sarah held my hand, gently.

"Alright I will give them another go."

We walked out. Paid the bill. Silent. No resistance left. Steroids again. Conform. Do as you are told.

Cream never arrived. Oozing sticky ointment instead. Steroids on, morning and night. No change.

Back into the steroid routine. Uncomfortable days and uncomfortable nights. I don't know how Sarah coped. I was just a zombie.

So started 2020. Awful. Endless. The nights were worse. Small hours especially. Silent tears. Hopelessness. Back in MMO11.

"Will I ever get my hands and feet back.?"

I didn't know. I *didn't know.* I didn't dare think about it.

A relentless rhythm.

Fucking, fucking fucking skin.

Try and stay positive.

Tiny improvements.

Tears.

Fucking, fucking fucking skin.

Try and stay positive.

Tiny improvements.

Tears.

I spent my life on the sofa.

I must have been hell to live with. I could do very little. Swinging from determination, optimism and despair.

SO: I'm very unhappy to report that I'm struggling to find any respite for my hands at the moment ... dry stinging, itchy sore they are doing it all whatever I do or put on them.

NB: Dear God Sue, so sorry to hear all this. Completely understand, now is not possible.

SO: Sorry I'd so wanted to Skype but I'm really struggling could do a few minutes perhaps

NB: ... of course you are struggling. This is impossibly infuriating on top of being painful & limiting for too feckin long ...

Sport always helped ...

SO: Phew ... watching FA cup live football in t-shirt and shorts with cotton 'elephants' wrapped round me

There were distractions

*SO: G&T hitting the spot with Abba **loud** cooking early supper*

Diary: Fiddled with lots of different creams for my hands... not helpful. Washed them a lot and it didn't improve things. Very aggravated by early evenings and I was driven to put steroid cream on earlier and earlier and possibly too much. My anxiety was rising daily. I needed anew strategy. I was tried all sorts to distract me. Meditation on Patience. Left wrist, very itchy. Calmed it with quiet. Only need a small amount of steroids each day. Do not be tempted to put more on to increase speed. Walking on Lancing Ring caused itching and pain on the inner balls of my feet. Ice and cream calmed them.

SO: Praise be I think this new treatment is beginning to work 😳 🤍

NB: *for treatment to continue to work* 🙏 ☺ *xxnb*

I kept hoping for improvement . Need to give myself permission to rest if I need to.

It was slow. SO very slow.

Watching Test cricket on TV always helped. The last time I had seen my dad was at Lords Cricket Ground when he was in a wheelchair following his stroke. I remembered.

CRICKET

Until my dad died, every January he would call.

"Do you want some tickets for the test match in June this year Susy?"

"Yes please. Who's playing?"

"It's the West Indies. I'll get seats in The Mound Stand."

"Brilliant!"

I started watching cricket with my dad in Garsdale. He loved his sport. Cricket, rugby union and football especially. We would settle into the small study with a black and white TV in the corner. Our telephone number was 1968 and I wondered if I would live to the year 1968. During his arthritis days when walking was difficult, cricket kept him going. I would sit with him. All through the uninterrupted coverage of a five day test match. But then there was watching live. At Lords. women couldn't be members. The unfairness didn't strike me until much later.

"I'll meet you outside the Grace Gate at 10.0am then we can take our time getting into our seats ready for the start at 11.00am."

"Which tube station?"

"St Johns Wood and then follow the crowd ... "

"I'll bring a pork pie and mini-rolls"

Ah mini-rolls. In a box of eight wrapped. Individual. Chocolate coated with cream middle and wrapped around sponge. We had them through moments in the day. A wicket. If we wanted a wicket. At lunch and tea breaks. To celebrate a hundred.

I still get a tingle up the back of my neck when I walk up stadium steps and see a field of play. Green pitch. Athletics track. Wembley. My dad's rolling gait slowed him down. His stick too. Uncomplaining. The odd grimace. I learnt to walk at his pace. He wouldn't queue. Boarding school entitlement.

In 1966 he took me to Wembley for the first time. The World Cup semi-final. England v Portugal. Walking up a packed Wembley Way to the old stadium. Jostling. Good natured. Big men walking. I could only see backs. Close. Watching, so I didn't loose my dad. Up long flights of stairs. A first glimpse of the pitch, the tingle born.

"It's so small! The pitch is so much smaller than I imagined."

"It's really green too. Wow. It's so exciting."

"Let's have a mini-roll."

Heart space. Watching live sport with my dad. In 1973 we had watched a rugby match together on TV. Barbarians v New Zealand. There was history to the match. NZ were the best. But this memory is not about that, it's raw emotion. A deep connection with my dad. Tears are in my eyes now as I write. Watching people play sport and going beyond what is possible. Wisps of joy with my rounders team at school. We saw the try live on TV, once. People now call it 'The Try'. From under their posts the Barbarians conjure up an unbelievable score.
"What a score!"

Tears flowed. Over the years, we described it to each other on the rare occasions it was replayed.

"I'm standing in Melbourne airport reading your airmail letter describing 'that' try with tears in my eyes."

There are many more. Sweet edges of remembrance, visceral moments. Fissures to my heart. Still powerful to hold him close.

DEPTHS

Now. Watching test cricket from South Africa. Live.

SO: Pope 100

NB: Yay!!!

Diary: Woken twice in the night with very dry hands. Morning both feet and hands were very dry so worked emollient in. Itching feet eased with cold and calm. Legs clear and calm. Legs generally better less redness and not itchy. By 5.0pm hands difficult nothing helped tried oat cream and Calendula ...

worse ... tingling and dry dry and painful looked ok though

A pint of Harvey's and Indian meal and a glass white wine didn't improve things. By 9.30pm exhausted with it ... FUCKING HANDS cream and steroids at 9.45-10.00pm

Yet, I kept hoping. Trying to notice the good, not so much the bad.

Try and stay positive.

Tiny improvements.

Tears.

Steroids.

Gloves.

Fucking, fucking fucking skin.

Try and stay positive.

Tiny improvements.

Gloves.

Tears.

Steroids.

I was still attempting to go to a singing group on Thursday morning. Determined.

"Are you OK Sue with your hands? You are still wearing gloves ..."

It didn't last.

SO: Morning ... struggling with skin again last night and over night, going to tuck in and be miserable today no choir and no therapy Sxx

NB: Oh no Sue 😟 😔 😢 that's so hard to hear & just not fair... do you see the doctor on Fri?

SO: Saw Dr yesterday ... She doesn't know much, just said I could keep on with steroids and gave me more cream, chilled last night and just dropped into tears and misery today ... xx

NB: ... of course you have dropped into tears & misery, bless you my dear pal, will light candles here for a turnaround today back on course of slow steady recovery xxnb 🙏 🖤 🖤

SO: ... 🙏 I've stopped trying to be brave and positive. Will tell A I'm tired and miserable when I get to therapy 🫠

SO: Resting quietly xx

NB: 🙏 🖤 🖤

Then something strange happened ...

SHAME

"I need to get to your spleen."

My trusted craniosacral therapist leant over and into my body. I was so distressed with hands and feet peeling and painful. She held my hands and I cried and shook. Her hands on my spleen.

"There is a lot of activity there. What do you think may be happening?"

"Oh I don't know ..."

I had sense of a deep and hidden knot of shame woven into my solar plexus.

"What might your spleen be telling you?

"... I've been silently, secretly sliding yellow green slime into your body…"

"How long do you think it's been doing that?"

"Possibly since I was about 14!"

I'm in tears now. Wrenching retching sobs. Pulled up by the roots. Unshed tears from way, way back. From walking wooden corridors. From wandering stairs. From summer days. From love lodged in the PE room.

Secret, silent, shame. Pumped into every cell.

"Breathe into it and see if we can begin to change the energy."

"What does the spleen do?"

"In simple terms it sets the formation of cell replication throughout the body."

"I think it has been hiding. *Doing it.* Since 1967."

I cried, I screamed, I struggled. I pulled its roots out.

Deep, deep underneath, a clear, centre. Warm positive. Me. Walking Tarka. Catch with my dad. Sculpture with mum. Before. Before.

I must nurture and support her to return. To skip.

Exhausted. I collapsed back home to my now familiar place on the sofa. Sarah endlessly, brilliantly supportive of me, handed me a cup of tea in my favourite blue pottery mug nicknamed "April" hand made by Emma Lacy[3]

"How are you doing there?"

I explained my session.

"Wow, that sounds really important."

It was. Eventually. At first I didn't link this session with my treatment. Like a crab in boiling water. I didn't jump out.

Patterns. Helpful psychologists say we repeat patterns in our lives. We fucking do. One of mine, which you may recognise, is to stay in an uncomfortable place and beat myself up for not moving sooner. Smell of burning martyr my father was prone to say. I knew that place.

SO: Sorry 😷 change of plan here ... f... king skin ... no improvement after the weekend and I need to check in with Specialist again as now into week 3 and legs and arms not much changed... I'm very brave most of the time ... will ring him in the morning Sxxx

NB: Ah feck Sue. Can't find words to say that could reach anything like what you must be feeling my dear pal. Sending you angel candle light, me into 7.15pm session shortly xxnb

SO: Have appointment with specialist at 11.45am 👍... had melt down earlier tonight but calmer now 😊

NB: Bless you Sue, hope you get some rest tonight & 🤞 for a helpful consultation with specialist tomorrow xxnb

---

[3] Emma Lacy: www.emmalacey.com

Diary: Melt down and panic attack this evening ... not very positive. Sarah is brilliant at calming me. Decided I will book in with Specialist again tomorrow.

"You are not taking enough steroids to make a difference!"

"You need to step up the ointment and go twice a day."

"I'll book you in for a punch biopsy."

"How do they do that?"

"They will cut out a disc of skin, with a punch, it heals quite quickly."

"Stitches?"

"Yes, and a local anaesthetic."

"Oh. So you don't know what it is ... ?"

"Mmm ... this will help us know."

I wonder ... I was beginning to know.

Steroid twice a day morning and evening. Difficult, very sticky and unpleasant. Using vinyl gloves to keep steroids working and hands moist. Wearing them at night. My journal records.

Craniosacral: in the session after my spleen. Something feels different. I begin to realise that my childhood despair and distress is not there as much. I feel stronger and less child like. I find myself speaking as an adult not as a child. A relief. Determination and resolve not distress. Much calmer and more in touch with here and now. Body responding to flow.

Despite this I'm really struggling. Will I ever get back to weaving or making anything? I can't hold a pen or even crayon to colour in. But I kept going ...

NB: Am hoping these past two days have been a little less challenging for you dear pal... but know this may not be the case. I know we may not catch up tomorrow so just a heads up if not raining, I'll play tennis at 11, & have Skype call at 4 xxnb

SO: Ah there ... I'm not doing too badly here most of the time ... how's about you drop me a text after tennis after lunch ? Sxx

NB: 👍 💚 Will do xxnb

SO: 🏐👀🏐👍💚

It didn't last. Like the tide. In and optimistic. Out with despair. Relentless. Trying. Cinema with Janet. Fell asleep in Dickens. Great film, pity I missed the middle. Feet and hands are sore with athlete's foot and cracking. Used fungal cream and bandage with antiseptic. Postponed our caravan collection until 29th Feb. No sign of weaving on the horizon. So boring.

Try and stay positive.

Tiny improvements.

Tears.

Steroids. Gloves.

Fucking, fucking fucking skin.

Try and stay positive.

Tiny improvements.

Gloves. Tears.

Steroids.

31st January Quiet day and Noelle check in. More of the same. 1st February. Skin stuff at 6.30-7.0 morning and night so my stickiness is reduced in bed. Am sleeping well despite this. Walking round the park. 4th February. Day of steady skin. Liked the value a friend gave to my shame root. Very powerful and helpful for me. Adults are vulnerable and frightened not always big and brave.

SO: 5th February: Into the 🛏 today. 👋 👋 🖐 🖐 😬 👍

NB: 👍 🖤

SO: 8th February: To Nymans Gardens alone for snowdrops.

With my mum.

SNOWDROPS

"It's always a long climb up to the Spring, Susy. The first snowdrop I see always lifts my spirits."

My mum's words came into my head that February morning. I was lying in bed. Gazing at the sky. Blue with wisps of cloud. Breezy. Cold. The routine of steroid cream on my hands, my feet, my shins and thighs completed. Again. Sticky. Stuck. Wait a minute ... No I fucking wasn't. I was going to find some snowdrops. Yes. *Yes*.

Extra coconut cream on my feet, between my toes.

"Malibu?... what are you up to?"

"I'm going to find some snowdrops ... where do you think I might see some, it's early?"

"Nymans might have them, when I volunteered there for the National Trust, where I made reindeers, the snowdrops were very early. February I think."

"Great. I'll use my Scottish National Trust card."

"Do you want me to come with you?"

"No, I'm going with my mum."

"OK. Take care and text when you get there."

"Will do."

Softest socks and trainers, loose. T-shirt, jumper, warm fleece, tracksuit bottoms. neck warmer, wool beanie, [my ears get cold first] gloves. Ready.

I drove gently. Not too much pressure.

The gravel was crunchy underfoot as I stepped out into the busy parking lot. Winter trees, bare, solid, waiting. All that potent energy flowing up the trunks pushing into the tips of branches ... into new leaves ... waiting to unfurl.

"Not yet, it's too fucking cold!"

Not the witch hazel though. I caught a scent, heady and sweet and tracked it to the row of small trees, more bushes in the dark soil. Yellow flowers. Amazing. I told mum. She knew about witch hazel, like her mum. Gardeners. After a warming coffee in the cafe I ventured out.

"Where will I find snowdrops, if there are any out yet?"

"Now, let me see. I think there are some. The best route might be north to the main gardens and then down the track towards to woodland. Follow the path over the lawn and through the small gate there. I think Eric said he saw some down there yesterday."

Down the track. Ice under hesitant foot. Nothing.

"Have you seen any snowdrops?"

"Yes ... there's a big patch of them just round the corners by those trees."

There they were. Hundreds ... I lay down next to them and wept.

SO: I've found them!!! Right down the track under the trees.

SHQ: Brilliant 🌿

Things were moving. Snowdrops helped. Cold paddling. A resolution. Power. No slime pumping. Crazy or what. After early morning tea I decided. *No more.* I wrote painfully in my journal with my favourite fountain pen. Strong words, my writing.

Today as a proud lesbian, creative artist, weaver and facilitator I have stopped putting steroids on my skin!!!

I had a bath, dressed. Used coconut cream on my feet and hands and no gloves. I am trusting my body and instincts to stop western medicine. At breakfast I told Sarah.

"I'm stopping steroids."

"OK ... what will you do instead?"

"Not sure yet ... Noelle rates acupuncture and I thought I might research Chinese medicine. I don't think I'll go for the biopsy either. I also want help for my soul, so I'm going to ask our lesbian pals to help me with films, books written by lesbians. Preferably positive, uplifting and funny."

Journal: I'm eating fruit and muesli with coffee ... At 9.25am my hands are tingling. Calendula not steroids on hands and feet and gloves 10.00am. Research begins.

SO: Morning 👯 last time we spoke you mentioned that your acupuncturists had said your energies were low during your thyroid investigations, it made me think 🤔 this weekend I have continued with steroids but they are having no positive effect possibly inflammatory to it all too ... So, yesterday after my Snowdrops and standing in the sea, I was in my pyjamas all day. I reviewed and did a bit of research again! I'm stopping steroids! Temperature of my skin, dampness, hot hands and feet, drying ... and then I remembered your comment and explored acupuncture, then into Chinese Medicine. I discovered a clinic with an international reputation for dermatology in Brighton (of course 😂) I rang this morning and my first task is to send a history & pictures + therapy, craniosacral medication etc so they can treat the whole body! That is my task this morning 👍 😍

NB: Woweeeeeeeee! I was in jammies all day yesterday too 😄 🙈! All the best with this Sue xxnb

They wanted EVERYTHING. Dates, times, emotions, treatments, medicines and why I thought my skin had reacted. My whole story. At last. Feels very exciting. Sent.

SO: I'm up for a 11.00 -11.30 meet ... 👍 took most of the day writing my story with dates, facts and observations + pictures. Sarah was brilliant with all the details and medication that I can't remember. Sent it at about 5.0pm so should hear tomorrow about the appointment.

SO: I've been putting steroids on my hands and feet for 40 days with the last 12 double doses! It's wild here. Sxxx

An appointment.

"Yes, we can help with this."

As I write now, I try to remember. This time has not always been so clear. Days ran into each other. A rhythm, possibly, but blurred like early morning mist. Horizon and detail indistinct. Moments ran into each other piling up with gloves, cream, brown herbs and resting. My threads of positivity were still there. I do wonder why. My love of cows noses. Rosebay Willow Herb. Grey armour. Jane. I don't have a skin condition; I had shame to shed.

After my appointment I made detailed daily notes. This *was* going to help. Stay with me here, it does get tedious.

It had been on a long journey. I hoped this was the last lap. Well, at least the beginning of the end. I recorded everything in my journal. Meticulously. Endlessly.

There were plenty of sceptics. Slow and steady. Chi is a bit low and depleted. Not surprising really. Bloods fine. Slowly, slowly. Calmness and compassion for myself. Softening. I was still very fragile. I had also started a scoring system for hands and feet 30 awful 0 healed.

Wednesday 12 February.
Appointment: circulation of blood a bit sluggish. System maybe tired. Liver good. Tongue bit dark. Likely that extremities may not get full nourishment and become dry and cracked. Eczema on hands and feet.
Hand and foot cream: very tender on first application. Wore gloves to be gentle. Collected herbal stuff. Twice a day, warm to body heat and drink before breakfast and supper 5 mins before meal. I can change to after a meal if needed.

SO: Paused therapy until skin healed. 😍

NB:

Bed time: red ointment on hands. Cream on soles. Both sore. Score today 30 both. More cream on hands and soles 4.00pm Palms very itchy but calmer after cream. Gloves on. Legs dry so put organic cocoa butter on them. 8.00pm hands have been tender also feet. Gloves back on. 10.00 Warm: slight new itching on upper thighs Score: Feet 29 Hands 29.

One week in. Definitely feel tiny improvements.

My spirits lifted. On the Sunday 23 February. I wrote.

My fingerprint has returned - first time since September. Gentle day.

Reading this now I can hardly believe it. So understated. The fight and anger gone. On the 27th February with scores of 18. I stopped making notes.

SO: ... woke up with soft hands this morning... 👍 😊 😊

NB ... soooo good to hear that Sue 😃 👍 👌 😊

SO ... one small step ...

Then I overdid it.

SO: Trip to Poole 👍 *However ... big flare up of skin as a result* 😖 *very early start and standing in cold didn't help my health either ... I have had a cough and tight chest over the weekend and now I'm trying to stay calm and tucked up. I'm not sure yet about tomorrow... a good night may render me well enough to travel but this is a heads up in case it doesn't* 😖 *Sorry sfoxx*

NB: Ah bless you Sue if you need a restful day just say I can always do some online cpd. Hopefully your skin will settle well soon, & lots of hot drinks for your chest/cold ... ah feck it... 😒 😟 😦 *. Xxnb*

SO: 👍 💜 Sarah just brought porridge for me and now I'm resting ... 😚
NB: 👍 😙

I dreamt about my dad at college, I had bronchitis and he took me home to Lancashire. I have a vague memory of my skin not being right then too. Mmmmm. The threads go way back.

Into March. First signs of Covid in the news. The week before first lock down, I make it out to lunch with a pal but she notices my hands are far from normal.

"God Susy, I didn't realise your hands were so bad."

23rd March 2020 Lock Down - I can do this. I've been locked down for months.

SO: Hi my dear ... sorry to miss your call ... I'm out of action this evening with difficult flare up of hands so just staying calm and resting ... will catch up tomorrow 💜 💜

NB: Very odd & unsettling times indeed dear pal. Hope the flare up has calmed since last night? 🤞 💜 Xxnb

SO: Yes a little ... managed a night without gloves and sox and slept a bit too. I'm really being challenged with routine calmness and compassion, patience... 🥰

NB: 💜 🙏 🤞 😇 😪

So much time in my life I have waited. Had patience. Waited to be brave enough to leave my marriage. Waiting to be brave enough to stand up and say "I'm a lesbian."

I had patience. Sarah reminds me that my weaving needs patience.

"All those threads. How many? Over 500 ... all threaded twice? How do you do that? Where do you get the patience?"

I had patience.

At a craniosacral session when I had begun my writing, Anna looked back at her notes.

Bit of spooky synchronicity 😀
April 4 2019 Told Anna I needed a new skin.
April 4 2020 Real sense of new skin 🙂😜💁

23RD MARCH 2020 COVID LOCKDOWN

What were you doing during first Covid lockdown?

SO: Not quite sure how to tell you this ... sit down with a large drink ... I have been working with my hands today and realised that I had not put "stuff" on them for a while ... AND IT WAS OK ... dry yes, but I could do things ... first time in 6 months. 😄😜💜💜💜

NB: 💜 👍😄💜🙏🌸🌿🌷🌹🌹😊

By May 2020 things were getting even better.

SO: Pleased to report two days glove free... I'm feeling like a dragonfly with my wings filling out slowly 💁💁

NB: Oooh that's a lovely image 😍💜 xxnb

SO: ... I'm doing hand sewing 😀 first time in months and months 😜

NB: 👍👍😀😍😊

Perhaps life and weaving were not too far away ...

CLOUDS

Such a difficult time. Separate. Skin. Isolated. Steroids. Both of us. My retreat into myself. Survival. Patience. Not much care or cuddling. *So* hard.

I didn't see it at first. I'd just been hurting, sitting on the sofa, sticky with steroids, watching sport, paddling in the sea, buying gloves, changing creams. Isolated. Oblivious. Then brown herbs. Then COVID.

"If we swing by the Clinic and go in and pick up your herbs, it's essential medication ... isn't it?"

Daily bulletins. Fear and indecision. Hand washing. Click and collect. Wiping tins and packets. Washing fresh food. Planning. Waiting. Isolated. No work. Clapping. Hearing dreadful news. Numbers dead. No cure or vaccination. Daily routines and online meetings took over.

I was so preoccupied with my skin and recovery. I didn't pay enough attention to Sarah or to life and love at home.

WRITING

In June 2020 with soft hands and nimble feet, my brain begins to function again. I decided that writing about my skin might be one way of making sense of it all. I had a taster day on a local creative writing course. Fiction and non-fiction. Enjoyed it and decided on a two year non-fiction creative writing course.

Now, I fell into the old hole again. Attempting to write about all the years of distress. I fell in again, deep. I would try to write about home or school or marriage and just get stuck. I needed to know more about this new pink skinned me. Was I different? This time eyes open. I put my pen down, stopped writing. Paused. Waited. Another Christmas.

I took my stories back to therapy. My pre-covid therapist had retired so a new one.

"I'm writing about a skin trauma and would like some help. I want a warm hand on the small of my back. I'd like an ally. Help with unpacking, understanding with sensing and feeling."

Over the weeks we began to unearth the softer, kinder, gentler me underneath. Took down more defences, recognised betrayals, validated my experiences. I explained to Sarah.

"You know when you talk about stuff you did in the 1980's, all the lesbian feminist action. I realise now, I found it hard to listen because I was so ashamed that I was married."

"I am beginning to pause and not punish myself so much. It's slow but I think I'm starting to like myself. Maybe it will let me be more caring towards you."

"I hope so."

Life and love softened. We drew closer. I paid attention. Tenderness returned. Clouds lifting. Slowly.

I continued to write. I learned.

"Perhaps I don't have to write about all of my life, perhaps only some bits of it?"

I planned, I plotted. I continued therapy to help me mine the trench and stack the finds. Each one. Each piece examined. Feeling it. Sensing it. I keep writing and sieving. A month ago with snowdrops up again. I wondered. Could I stop? Had I done enough therapy for now?

ENDINGS

Now there's another pattern I can't avoid. Endings. Early life training gave me the "wrench and tear don't feel it" model. The first thick layer of my shell. I knew how to do it, so until recently made sure that was the only model I used. Now I could try another way.

I asked my therapist if I could have fortnightly sessions, not weekly.

"I don't do fortnightly."

"Oh."

So with all the courage I could muster, with heart beating, I took a breath in and said ...

"I think then, I would like to finish therapy for now and do a sensitive ending."

Breathe out.

"That sounds good. Let's make it two weeks so we can review and go slowly with our ending."

I've done one week. Validation, softness, care. My shell is softening to skin. I'm looking forward to next week.

Today, I woke up the right way up. Not face down exploring my past life, but facing upwards into the morning sky. Facing my future, not my past. Allowing the creative me to flourish. I now know I can write, but today I decided to live my present not my past.

EPILOGUE

Morning in the Downs
To be alive.
Up here effortlessly, a new feeling.
Weight of tangled insecurities and doubt lifted.
Fleet of foot and hand now.
Thinking more of metaphors than breakfast.
Ancient downland curves effortlessly green, intoxicating silent.
To be alive to this moment holds me
close to memories of family gone.
How can it be so beautiful, so long,
so gentle, so many summers past?
To be alive.

Today, I'm beginning a new weaving. Winding the warp. The first practical stage of weaving. After weeks of design, colour lines and puzzling. Putting reds with oranges and a fleck of yellow. Does it need navy? Should that blue bamboo go there, or would the pale blue wool be better? After many hours. With the sett and the shape. With tie up and threading. With a colour pallet. I've decided. I know what I am going to do. A wide scarf. Bespoke. I'm about to begin the winding of a new warp. It will be over 400 threads. I need soft hands and a clear head. Feeling, sensing, holding the yarns. I can do that now. Each thread, parallel, separate, and the right length. Painting with threads. How do I do it? I don't really know, even now after ten years. Very very carefully and with patience. I am learning to love each and every stage.

Just like the threads of my life that I've gathered. Sailing, poetry, facilitator, baskets and weaving. Ah yes, weaving. All more untangled, valued now. Wrong pattern. Too tight and constricting. Shame. Deadly. Eased. Much easier on myself now. I'm learning to love myself at last.

I print off the pattern. Each thread, numbered. Each colour, decided. First a thread guide. Essential. Warp length and extra for wastage. Four metres this one. Cotton non stretch. A bright colour unlike my warp colours. I wind it to show the way. Especially the crosses. Crosses are for keeping threads separate, tied just a few inches from the ends of the warp so that the yarns cross and stay separate for threading.

Crosses
Keeping separate
Round three small beams
Making a cross
Going down inside then up
Coming up outside then down
Alternate, cross
Stay separate
Every time
Concentration
Top and bottom
Where alternate threads cross over
Keep separate
Parallel weaving
Help each thread
Stay separate
Every time
Miss one, disaster
Every time
No cross, everyone, everything falls apart
Weeks of work, metres of thread, heartbreak and rage
Crosses are important
Stay separate.

Guide thread on. Winding a warp. It's like sailing a boat in a breeze. Concentration. Rhythm. Timeless joy and ease. Small acts of rebellion, sailing, kept me alive back then. Still in denial, deep in the closet but somehow threads of freedom and creativity showing through. Deep blue probably.

Back to my warp. I am settled into my studio. A big space. Upstairs at the front of the house looking out over the avenue with a glimpse of the sea. A quiet space. Bookcases stacked with yarns, merino and bamboo. And my beautiful Scandinavian floor loom. There, huge, fantastic. During my weaving diploma I had wondered if I might take over the front bedroom for weaving. Taking space for myself was still a new feeling. Would Sarah mind? Of course she wouldn't. She was encouraging.

"Sounds like a good idea to me."

So here I am in my studio. Comfortable. Right clothes, right socks, right breakfast. A clear day ahead. Carousel in space on a small table on the floor in front of me. Easy sitting and spinning height. Room to flow, to rotate and to move. Room for the cones of thread. A mixture of merino wool and bamboo for softness. Pattern on a clipboard. Soft pencil sharpened. Scissors. A play or story to listen to. Interesting but not distracting.

Begin. Loop over the top bar. Spin. Over under round. Top cross behind. Wind and spin. Wind a spin. Over under round. Bottom cross behind. Round end post. Spin the other way. Under and over round. Bottom cross front. Cross established. Pattern. Wind and spin. Wind and spin. Keep tension. Under and over round. Top cross front. Cross established. Pattern. Round top end post. Repeat. Repeat. Spin and repeat. After groups of 10 stop. Mark off on the pattern and the number. Remember to cross the counting thread. Soft pencil. Check colours. Count. Check. Begin again. An hour then a break. Another hour. A day. I will weave two warps of 200 threads each. Carefully tying the warp along its length like a sausage. And even more carefully with a bright distinctive yellow cotton, I will tie the crosses across the centre to hold them secure, separate and mark the place before and after them. Make them visible and very secure. Crosses are so important.

Slowly, slowly, I take my day's work off the carousel folding the warp over my hands into a loose chain and I lay it down carefully.

Time for a cup of tea and a walk on the beach. That's the first stage. Done.

Bio

Sue Orton is a writer, poet, and handweaver.

She lives with Sarah, her partner, on the West Sussex coast, between the South Downs and the sea. Sailing and singing have always been important parts of her life.

Sue's professional career has been devoted to helping people learn, develop, and thrive together. Her first book (co-authored), *Groupwork Practice in Social Work*, is now in its third edition.

Sue's weaving is inspired by place. Her South Downs tweed was developed over the course of many walks.

You can explore more of Sue's writing, poetry and weaving at www.sueorton.co.uk